# Academic Freedom
# and the Inclusive University

*Edited by Sharon E. Kahn*
*and Dennis Pavlich*

# Academic Freedom
# and the Inclusive University

**UBC**Press · Vancouver · Toronto

Printed in Canada on acid-free paper ∞

ISBN 0-7748-0807-1

---

**Canadian Cataloguing in Publication Data**

Kahn, Sharon E., 1946
   Academic freedom and the inclusive university

   Includes index.
   ISBN 0-7748-0807-1

   1. Academic freedom. 2. University autonomy. 3. Inclusive education. I. Kahn, Sharon E., 1946- II. Pavlich, Dennis J.

LC72.A44 2000          378.1'21          C00-910779-7

---

UBC Press acknowledges the financial support of the Government of Canada through the Book Publishing Industry Development Program (BPIDP) for our publishing activities.

Canadä

We also gratefully acknowledge the support of the Canada Council for the Arts for our publishing program, as well as the support of the British Columbia Arts Council.

The quotation appearing on pages 99-100 has been reprinted with permission, © world copyright by Schocken Publishing House Ltd., Tel Aviv, Israel.

UBC Press
University of British Columbia
2029 West Mall, Vancouver, BC V6T 1Z2
(604) 822-5959
Fax: (604) 822-6083
E-mail: info@ubcpress.ubc.ca
www.ubcpress.ubc.ca

# Contents

# Academic Freedom and Inclusivity: A Perspective
*Dennis Pavlich*

When internal conflicts plunge academic communities into controversy, the line thought to distinguish campus calm from the commotion of the "real" world disappears. Although some campus disputants would claim to maintain a high level of objectivity and may even do so, others barely disguise a discourse activated by rhetorical invention. "Secluded" and "detached" are words not easily associated with the name-calling, loaded language, skewed evidence, and convoluted logic that sometimes characterize campus conflict.

It follows, then, that in the course of such conflicts many – partisan and bystander alike – will deplore such conflicts, not only as obstructing the authentic work of the university, but also as threatening the ideology of the institution as a place in society where knowledge of social change can be studied from a distance and objectively assessed. Yet it is precisely when a university community fiercely debates endemic issues that it engages in one of its most important tasks. Such controversies, however disagreeable to participant and observer, stimulate the critical self-examination essential for rejuvenation of a kind that otherwise meritorious institutional structures and procedures, whose goal is to maintain equilibrium, work to prevent.

The university is thus both of the world and separate from it, and the durability of this 850-year-old institution may result from its paradoxical ability to draw back from direct involvement in extramural skirmishes and simultaneously to enact those skirmishes intramurally and no less fiercely on its own grounds and terms, and for its own purposes. Such enactment occurred in more recent times during the anti-Communist frenzy of the 1950s, the counterculture revolt of the 1960s, the feminist movement of the 1970s, and the human rights crusade of the 1980s. Offering yet another chapter in the long history of such skirmishes, the essays in this book represent even more recent conflicts between self-proclaimed defenders of academic freedom and the proponents of inclusive learning environments. The sides in this debate advance a rhetoric forged in contemporary politics both on and off campus, and no wonder: academic freedom and the inclusive university are crucial issues to scholars, for whom the life of the mind is inseparable from the matter of daily life.

The university is not just another workplace. As Bernard Shapiro notes in his chapter, universities constitute "one of society's central, defining institutions." And so, when the literature and media, both internal and external to the university, speak of it as "in crisis" or "in ruins," the academy needs to take a hard look at itself. It should review fundamental values, how and for what reason they were acquired, how they are protected, and whether they should be reshaped to adjust to newer values, norms, and institutional changes that are emerging in our society.

One such set of characterizing interests, and one of the two on which this book focuses, is that students and faculty should challenge conventional university values, norms, and practices and also tolerate and respect classmates' and colleagues' defence of the status quo. "Academic freedom" is the nomenclature used for the modern idiom of this fundamental ideology and accompanying set of values. Academic freedom establishes the high moral ground from which the university community speaks, for it endorses as a principle and as a desired *modus operandi* within the academy the requirement of integrity and minimization of personal interest in utterances relating to teaching and research. This moral ground is steeped in romance and myth. Scholars and members of the university community look back with admiration to the "golden age" of Pericles, when independent thinkers committed themselves to ideals of free inquiry and free speech. Later, Socrates, Aristotle, and Plato are thought to have bestowed the legacy that sustained medieval European universities' search for knowledge through political, social, and religious upheavals that also constrained free inquiry and closed minds. Paradoxically, Roman Catholic and Protestant churches are depicted as imperilling the growth of freedom to inquire and express the results of it. Until the twentieth century, religious affiliation and belief were determinative factors of university character, and yet they also fostered the ideas of religious tolerance and liberty that marked the triumph of the Enlightenment. Again, in an even earlier age, scholasticism had tried to liberate the world from the tyranny of superstition by civilizing a feudal world with Plato, Aristotle, and new interpretations of the Bible. It also had the effect of supporting the autonomy of the church and its freedom to express views on spiritual matters objectionable to secular authorities. By the same token, universities sponsored by secular authorities checked slavish obeisance to church dogma. The ideas and values underlying this history have broadened into the nomenclature of academic freedom. They are seemingly supported by notions of university autonomy and entrenched by tenure, and have become the taken-for-granted protection of all professors, part of the assumptive framework of the university lives of faculty and students.

The past two hundred years are less susceptible to romanticizing the evolution of academic freedom, perhaps because that evolution merged with the proclamation of individual freedoms that quickened with the American Revolution and the Bill of Rights. Less accessible to easy mythologizing, the history of the late nineteenth and early twentieth centuries reveals religious and civil freedom – noticeable in the charters of some early American colleges – advancing to a point where the professional associations of the professoriate adapt prevailing civil liberties to the world of the academy. Academic freedom in North America is a function of the march to progressive civil liberties and the professionalization of the professoriate, the latter having commenced in Europe in the late eighteenth century at the Universities of Göttingen and Leiden. The faculty at Göttingen had sedulously fostered the view that detachment was a prerequisite of objective scholarship. Freedom of speech and inquiry became tools in the hands of a special class of academic professionals, who, even in the humanities, became scientists using methods of neutral investigation and dispassionate appraisal of the facts. The role of academic freedom in this methodology is presupposed and has become familiar in its twentieth-century vernacular. However, the core notions of free inquiry and expression have taken forms more or less compatible with the academic methodologies of social worlds other than the democratic, liberal ones that define the nation state in which we live.

If late-nineteenth-century history tends to strip romance and myth from academic freedom and to represent its modern evolution as progressing alongside religious and civil freedom, academic freedom does not now come unadorned, for it has become its own myth: an icon to be revered above all else, an article of faith, an essentialist doctrine bearing pontifical force. Used as cliché, academic freedom can be applied to justify conduct as obvious and without the need for further questioning; somewhat similar to the role of the nineteenth-century cliché "manifest destiny," which successive American administrations used to great effect to justify the colonization of North America. The cliché status of a phrase prevents meaningful dialogue by camouflaging a challengeable position with the simple utterance of the iconic trump. For example, the media and others sometimes use "threat to academic freedom" or "political correctness" to put an issue beyond debate. And yet acceptance of the strong values that form the basis of the idea of academic freedom should not be the means of suppressing meaningful criticism and debate about the scope of its application. This debate is a continuing one, and there is no obvious reason why principle should preclude a resolution that takes issues of inclusion into consideration in formulating a useful meaning of the phrase. "Academic freedom" as icon masks the changing social and political circumstances that compel adaptation of meaning without transforming a central notion. But academic freedom is not a static and absolute idea.

Were university structures, populations, and curricula frozen in time, the iconic status of academic freedom and questions about the scope of its application might, by and large, prove nonproblematic. However, the changing organization of how universities do business, and the different constituencies that now demand a voice in shaping that administration, have required renewed reassessment of some of the fundamental values of the university to consider how they should best coexist with emerging values and social norms.

The latter half of the twentieth century witnessed massive changes in the scope, composition, and administration of universities. In the early 1950s, many small or medium-sized academic institutions began growing into mega-universities composed of heterogeneous populations and fragmented fields of study that strained the notion of scholarly communities and shared values. The massive scale of such institutions accentuates contradictions characteristic of public universities: anti-elitist, yet part of the new elite; antipower, yet seeking to join society's power brokers. Part of the explanation for this phenomenon is the apparent merger of the university into the state apparatus and, broadly speaking, its policy objectives. The values and processes of the state have become so widely accepted and shared by administrators, professors, and students that integration into the affairs of the universities has sometimes, though not always, been seamless. This integration may explain the apparently ready acceptance by the academy of extensive regulation of its economy (tuition fees, for example) and social norms (human rights codes and environmental systems of permits, for instance). The university has, to a significant degree, come to rely on the instrumentalist-oriented state to protect free speech and policy matters that the general community accepts as social progress, including the elimination of social exclusion and deprivation. The scope of the university's autonomy has become a matter of political negotiation within the parameters set by the state. Academic freedom is part of that process. So is the politics of recognition.

The modern large university is akin to a city with multifaceted managerial and hierarchical structures and governance arrangements that superintend, control, and regulate groups of people reflecting the diversity of cultures and subcultures of contemporary Canadian society. Ten times more students enroll in universities today than before the Second World War, and those students come not only from the upper class but also from the middle, labouring, and under classes. They represent backgrounds of differing ethnicity, race, culture, religion, and physical ability. University faculties and staffs are marked by similarly diverse profiles. Attempts to assimilate the university to reflect the greater community are not only a part of social morality but also a byproduct of forging partnerships with the giant bureaucracies of our times – municipal, provincial, and federal governments –

and the accompanying regulatory constraints imposed by them. As well, such alliances have incorporated other major centres (and sources) of power and wealth: large corporations, foundations, and wealthy citizens. Industry ties with universities are now commonplace.

Coalitions, especially those that are financially advantageous, come with a price. External demands for university accountability and transparency are at a very high level, with the result that everything is tracked: access, assets, curriculum, environments, finances, governance, growth, research, and teaching as well as faculty, staff, and student backgrounds and diversity. Technology facilitates accountability efforts and more revolutionary possibilities for the future. Outcomes such as student success in the job markets and measurements have become integral to the planning and regulation they presuppose. To complicate matters, universities, like most modern organizations, have succumbed to the *nouveau* socializing mythology that state policy (and, therefore, university policy) works best when the methods and expectations that emulate the axioms of economics and commerce drive it. Accordingly, the culture of business, with its entrepreneurial doctrines adumbrating commodities, competition, flexibility, management, market-like efficiencies, and partnering, and much else, occupy the attention of writers and advisors who argue the role of universities as "change agents" in the new "global economy." "Customer satisfaction," "branding," "products," and similar epithets have crept into the working jargon of universities, revealing the incorporation of this "new way of thinking" in university operations and planning. The culture of business is pervading global cultures, too, complicating debate on the relationship of new to older values and practices. Of course, alignment with prevailing orthodoxies or "forms of life" is not new for universities. They have always been able to adapt – sometimes in profound ways, always with difficulty – to fit dominant expectations, whether the Reformation-induced paradigms of the sixteenth and subsequent centuries, or the tilt toward nationalism that characterized Western societies in the first half of the twentieth century. In both instances, the language matched the social conventions of the form.

The redefinition of universities by the state has not precluded the academy from an important role in helping to craft the workings of the liberal democratic state. The twentieth-century success of the implementation of the regulatory apparatus as a means of effecting social progress is indebted to the development of this ideology within the universities and the students who have graduated from this teaching. "Progressive" bureaucrats and legislators were exposed to the ideas and values of mentors and teachers imbued with the works of Marx, Weber, Keynes, Rawls, and, more recently, Friedmann, and notions of government instrumentation for the welfare of the people. The "third way" debate, so well articulated by the vice chancellor of the London School of Economics, continues along the path of redefining the nature of the state as one with less government and regulation. However, this diffusion does not seriously detract from the basic power of the nation state as the primary organizing force of our society.

The contemporary alignment of the academy with state and commerce has had far-reaching implications for the autonomy of the university – always, at best, a relative concept. Dispute resolution affords an interesting illustration. Like the church, universities are no longer cloistered outside the fabric of the state and its apparatus. In an earlier era, recourse to an external authority such as the courts was relatively unusual, outside of tort and breach of contract lawsuits with third parties. Disputes arising with the university were handled within the institution using processes with final appeal to the Chancellor or the Visitor, persons who enjoyed high status in the community and had close links with the university. Today, universities are increasingly involved in a multiplicity of types of adjudications, with many disputes handled by an assortment of arbiters unconnected to the university, using processes effectively mandated by the state and monitored by its court system. As the new chief justice of Canada has observed, the state system increasingly transforms social and political issues into legal questions necessitating court or judicial-like processes. Inevitably, the role of the Visitor, for example, has been in steady decline through disuse and rests in oblivion in many jurisdictions. Instead, the services of external professionals are used to conduct inquiries, act as ombudsmen, mediate, arbitrate, or serve on specialized quasi-judicial administrative councils such as labour and environment boards, human rights tribunals, and other regulatory panels. For instance, in the 1990s at UBC, the decisions of external arbitrators from private practice or the public tribunal system have sometimes provoked controversy on (and off) campus. The recommendation of a private investigator to suspend admission of graduate students to the Department of Political Science and the decision of the BC Human Rights Tribunal in *Mahmoodi* v. *The University of British Columbia* are recent illustrations. University practices have been hegemonized by the state with the result that its methods of dispute resolution have also been adopted by, and become routine, in university systems and policies. "Due process" is part of the stock of phrases of the university community and as a measure, purportedly incorporated into policy and practice. Where due process has not been incorporated or inadequately addressed rulings by university decision makers have been severely criticized.

These developments have resulted in the establishment at many universities of in-house legal departments that service the contract, employment, human rights, student discipline, risk management, and due diligence needs of the institutions. The function goes well beyond the syndic and parallel models, and resembles general counsel in government or large corporations. Administrative quasi-judicial bodies, or their look-alikes in the academy, are sometimes perceived within the universities as possessing imperfect knowledge and appreciation of the complex value system underlying the teaching and research of a university in the framework of a community of scholars. Where this perception is widespread, decisions rendered by such external bodies, and perceived by a large segment of the professoriate as externally imposed, cause enormous tension within the academy. This outcome is, of course, a contradiction, because the state dispute-resolution system, both court and arbitration alike, comes as an important part of the state value system that the academy has systematically absorbed, sometimes willingly (and often for good reasons) but for the most part passively and uncritically.

Major components of the contemporary state value system are free speech *and* equal opportunity for all its citizens, including access to the education system and the job market to which it has become tied. Access to, participation in, and increased accountability to serve all cultures and subcultures in Canada have brought into sharp focus the need for universities to reflect and be representative of those communities. This goal, along with effective state demands to plan achievement of social equity, has engendered confrontations on how issues of "inclusivity" are to be effected within the academy. How should the changing cultural composition of faculty, staff, and students affect the values that form the foundation of learning and research? To what extent are those values, connected as they are with free speech, enhanced or limited by juxtaposing them with the values of the business community and its emphasis on customer satisfaction? Do accountability, inclusivity, and dependency on external authority undermine traditional university values, including autonomy, freedom of inquiry, and freedom of expression? Is the value of freedom of speech, now congruent with state objectives, already protected by labour legislation and developing administrative law? Is this protection sufficient? If access to and proper accommodation of different cultural groups within Canadian society is an important social policy objective of the state, does it matter that for some identity groups offensive speech acts may be a disincentive to accessing the university and its learning? Should the academy autonomously assemble the priorities of its value system with selective homage to the state's high priority in the sphere of communitarianism and social justice? These questions may not exhaust the issues concerning the university "in crisis" or "in ruins." Moreover, are they the relevant ones with respect to free speech, access, and social progress within the academy? If not, which are?

In 1996, to focus debate on the issues associated with these questions, David W. Strangway, then president of UBC, invited the Alma Mater Society, the Graduate Student Society, and the Faculty Association to cosponsor a national conference. "Academic Freedom and the Inclusive University" was held at UBC on 10-12 April 1997. This book evolved from that event.

## Part 1: Clarifying Concepts in Language, Law, and Ideology

Discouraging the easy expectation that the definition of key terms facilitates debate, *Stanley Fish* argues that terms like "academic freedom" and "inclusive university" have no absolute value; rather, they are political weapons masquerading as abstract principles. Although their proponents tend to treat these concepts as self-evident and absolute, Fish helps us understand that these honorifics enable conduct directly counter to the ideals they promote. Proponents of academic freedom seek to deny that freedom to those who would limit freedom of speech, just as advocates of the inclusive university seek to deny participation by those who reject the principles of inclusion.

Like Fish, who writes out of his American experience, *Frederick Schauer* takes pains to clarify the distinction between American and Canadian concepts of freedom of speech. Schauer shows us that in the United States, academic freedom affirms the freedom of speech guaranteed in principle to all Americans, whereas in Canada, academic freedom is an exemption extended to academics from otherwise applicable supervisory requirements. Like Fish, Schauer has reservations concerning the value of academic freedom.

In the final chapter of Part 1, *Lynn Smith* attempts a solution to the conceptual difficulties created by the terms "academic freedom" and "inclusive university." She advocates that we seek to create an atmosphere of mutual respect by redefining concepts so that we may achieve a harmony necessary for progress toward the greater good of the university.

## Part 2: The Changing Culture

The next five authors study the conflict between academic freedom and the inclusive university from the perspectives of theoretical positions, historical surveys, and personal experience. Disinterested in debating the pros and cons of inclusion, *Bernard Shapiro* puts it plainly: Universities have a civic function that requires them to open their doors to all, even if there is an uproar on university campuses over inclusion. Shapiro argues that liberalism as advocated by some jeopardizes that ideal of inclusion.

*Jennie Hornosty* agrees with Shapiro, but she goes further, arguing that academic freedom is an outgrowth of liberal theory that privileges individuals over their social matrix and, thus, seeks to conceal the principle that human beings first and foremost bear social identities. Hornosty proposes that healing the current rift on university campuses requires that the liberal concept of academic freedom be brought into harmony with a concept of diversity and inclusion based on the idea of the "social individual."

The final three chapters in Part 2 provide historical and personal perspectives on the nature and impact of the changes taking place on Canadian campuses. *Michiel Horn* provides an extensive history of the sexism and racism that restricted the opportunities for women and minorities to participate in the intellectual life of Canadian universities. *Judy Rebick* describes her experiences in Canadian universities, exemplifying the sexism and racism that are still found on Canadian campuses. Rebick also touches on the lack of coherent direction of these institutions, a theme echoed by *Stan Persky*, who castigates university administrators for promoting academic programs of dubious value and chides his colleagues for their inability to construct a coherent antiharassment policy.

## Part 3: Academic Freedom in Peril

The chapters in Part 3 argue that the promotion of inclusion on university campuses has destroyed a consensus essential for legitimate academic life. *John Fekete* suggests that the inclusive university and academic freedom are incompatible entities. He would prefer that the former be called the "intrusive university" for its disruptive influence on academic freedom. In agreement, *Graham Good* warns that identity politics' emphasis on women and minorities has undermined the liberal university, which traditionally upheld the value of individualism. Also concerned with issues of ideology, *Harvey Shulman* closely examines the uproar following the appointment of a non-Jew to the directorship of a Queens College Judaic studies program in New York. Shulman implies that academic freedom flourished until recent times when the inclusion of large numbers of women and minorities transformed North American campuses both demographically and intellectually. In an analysis of student evaluations, *Stanley Coren* demonstrates how a mechanism designed to promote inclusion by exposing racism and sexism threatens the status and authority of faculty.

## Part 4: Theoretical and Practical Challenges to the Inclusive University

The five chapters in Part 4 focus on theoretical and practical problems that arise as universities seek to promote inclusion. *Diane Dyson,* in a case study, analyzes issues that arose when a Christian fundamentalist accused a professor of harassment. Dyson's article illuminates dilemmas for which current university practices – those that support academic freedom and those that seek to protect minority rights – do not provide easy answers.

Although *Marie Fleming* believes that creating an inclusive university is a worthwhile goal, she warns the reader that feminist theories privileging women's experience undermine efforts to build inclusive perspectives on human experience. *Jennifer Bankier* focuses on how the civic function of universities is defined in part by their subservience to federal and provincial law. From a perspective informed by her years of experience in faculty associations, which must conform to regulations, Bankier concludes that academic freedom and the inclusive university are designed to address the reality and the legitimacy of individual and social identities. *Lorna Marsden* argues that the institution of externally imposed harassment officers on campus stifles the traditional role of academic debate in faculties and senates. And in the closing chapter, *Dorothy Smith* traces the chilly climate concept to its source in in-group/out-group contrasts and recommends a strategy for achieving the mutual respect she contends is the prerequisite for successful academic debate.

In their discussions of the role of academic debate, the last two chapters give voice to the belief that all the chapters in this book silently express: it is through the energy, insight, scholarly detachment, and emotional commitment of men and women participating in academic debate that universities move forward.

The university "in crisis" or "in ruins" is a dramatic call for the academy to reflect on the meaning of its primary values for use in the twenty-first century. Ronald Barnett, noted scholar in the field of higher education, suggests some likely methods of approach: "Those of a postmodern turn of mind will urge the notion of deconstruction; those more in a managerialist mode might urge the notion of reconstruction. But in an age of supercomplexity, the idea of construction should not be lightly abandoned." As history shows, social, political, and economic forces within the communities served by universities favour construction – doubtlessly, one that is strongly influenced by their will. But a community is best served by a university that defends its independence to determine its own directions. This determination can only be arrived at and convincingly explained through independent debate. The discussion in these pages examines an important set of issues that need to be addressed if that construction is to prove successful and enduring: the significance, value, and meaning of the relationship between academic freedom and the inclusive university.

### References

Barnett, Ronald. 2000. *Realizing the University*. Philadephia, PA: Open University Press.
Berlinerblau, Jacques. 1999. *Heresy in the University*. New Brunswick, NJ: Rutgers University Press.
Compayre, Gabriel. 1983. *Abelard and the Origin and Early History of Universities*. London, UK: William Heinemann.
Giddens, Anthony. 2000. *The Third Way and its Critics*. Cambridge, UK: Polity Press.
McEwen, Joan I. 1995. "Report in Respect of the Political Science Department of the University of British Columbia." Vancouver: University of British Columbia.
*Mahmoodi* v. *The University of British Columbia*. 1999. BCHRTD 52.
Neilson, William, and Chad Gaffield, eds. 1986. *Universities in Crisis*. Montreal: Institute for Research on Public Policy.
Readings, Bill. 1996. *The University in Ruins*. Cambridge, MA: Harvard University Press.
Russell, Conrad. 1993. *Academic Freedom*. London, UK: Routledge.
Schmitt, Charles, ed. 1981. *History of Universities*. Vol. 1. Earls Barton, UK: Nene Litho.

# Part 1
# Clarifying Concepts in Ideology, Language, and Law

# 1
# What's Sauce for One Goose: The Logic of Academic Freedom
*Stanley Fish*

All my life I've been searching for a position no one likes, and I may have found it. It goes like this: Academic freedom is the name of a way of thought that confuses eccentricity with genius and elevates pettiness, boorishness, and irresponsibility to the status of virtue; evacuates morality by making all assertions equivalent and, because equivalent, inconsequential; empties history of its meaning so that actions proceeding from entirely different motives and agendas become indistinguishable as instances of individual preference and free choice; and promotes a regime of relativism by refusing to make judgments, on the reasoning that one man's meat is another man's poison. It is this last – one man's meat is another man's poison – that makes the whole thing work. It is a complex argument: first, it asserts fallibility. We are all prone to error and to the overvaluation of our own opinions. From fallibility follows the obligation to refrain from judging one another: Who among us is fit to cast the first stone? From the obligation to refrain from judging one another follows an ethic of mutual respect: Because none of us is God and in full possession of the truth, we must allow others the freedom to pursue the truth by their own rights, and they must allow us to do the same. In Kantian terms, this ethic becomes the doctrine of the autonomy of free agents who are to be regarded not as means but as ends. The final flower of the entire sequence is the logic of reciprocal rights. If I claim a privilege – say, the privilege of speaking my mind without restrictions – I must accord the same privilege to my fellow autonomous agents; and if I seek to restrain the speech or action of my fellows, I must accept the same restraint on my own speech and action. In Kant's words, "Each may seek his happiness in whatever way he sees fit so long as he does not infringe upon the freedom of others to pursue a similar end; that is, he must accord to others the same rights he enjoys himself."[1] Or in the words of John Stuart Mill: "We must beware of admitting a principle of which we should resent as a gross injustice the application to ourselves."[2]

It would be hard to overestimate the power of this line of reasoning, which underwrites such familiar statements as "You can't fight discrimination with discrimination," "Racism is racism, no matter what the colour, ethnicity, or economic status of the perpetrator," "Speech should be freely allowed even when, no, especially when, we find the message loathsome," "What's sauce for the goose is sauce for the gander." These and similar pronouncements are seldom inquired into – they constitute the limit of the open inquiry they otherwise mandate – but I propose to inquire into them with a view toward rendering them less comfortable than you may now find them; and I will begin with what might seem an unlikely topic, religion and religious discourse, which are to my mind the keys to understanding academic freedom, at least as it developed in the United States. I say this because of a famous passage in the declaration of principles of the American Association of University Professors (AAUP), first published in 1915 and left in place (if only by silence) in subsequent declarations. In that passage, the AAUP denies to religiously based institutions the name of "university" because "they do not, at least as regards one particular subject, accept the principles of freedom of inquiry." Such institutions, the association grandly allows, may continue to exist, "but it is manifestly important that they should not be permitted to sail under false colors," for "genuine boldness and thoroughness of inquiry, and freedom of speech, are scarcely reconcilable with the ... inculcation of a particular opinion upon a controverted question."[3] It is not that controverted questions should not be asked, but answers to them should not be presupposed and insulated from the challenge of free rational inquiry.

Unfortunately, it is the nature of religious dogma to resist and even condemn challenges from perspectives other than its own. Accordingly, in an institution founded on dogma, some avenues of inquiry may have been closed off even before the classroom doors open. As Professor Walter Metzger puts it, "Academic freedom ... was historically the enemy and is logically the antithesis of religious tests."[4]Although the dangers to unfettered inquiry can have many more sources – in legislative actions, administrative biases, and forms of political pressure including what has come to be known as "political correctness" – religion has always been considered the original and prototypical danger, and the fact that it is a danger whose force has diminished in the wake of the Enlightenment makes it a convenient reference point for its modern successors. Thus, Philip Resnick of the University of British Columbia speaks of the "long and hard struggle for the freedom of scientific inquiry ... against very strong opposition from the adherents of religious orthodoxy" before going on to consider more recent threats from powerful economic interests and various forms of identity politics. And in *Moral Panic: Biopolitics Rising,* John Fekete characterizes the emergence of campus speech codes as "The New Religion"; speech codes are shots fired in a "holy war" in which universities are pushed in the direction of becoming "doctrinal institutions" bent on punishing "heresies" that deviate "from orthodox beliefs." This outcome, Fekete goes on to say, is "the *fundamentalism* of biopolitics," the "new piety," a form of Calvinism not unlike the Inquisition, all leading to a creed-state "on the model of medieval Christendom."[5]

What makes these statements somewhat odd is that whenever freedom is celebrated, freedom of religion is always high on the list of what the concept includes. Here is a sentence from an essay on academic freedom by the legal philosopher Ronald Dworkin: "Freedom of speech, conscience, and religion, and academic freedom are all parts of our society's support for a culture of independence and of its defense against a culture of conformity."[6] Notice that religion occupies opposing positions in the two halves of this sentence: in the first half, it is one of the freedoms; in the second, it is, implicitly, the enemy of freedom because of its insistence on conformity (with doctrine, or received morality, or rigid theodicy). Of course, in standard liberal thought this paradox – religion is honoured, religion is condemned – is easily resolved by invoking the belief/action distinction, as the Supreme Court of the United States did when it rejected the claim by some Mormons that polygamy was essential to their religion and thus protected by the free exercise clause. "Laws are made for the government of actions, and while they may not interfere with mere religious belief and opinions, they may with practices."[7] That is, Mormons are free to believe and say anything they like so long as they do not put their beliefs and words into actions of which the authorities disapprove. One sees in this example what freedom of religion means in a liberal regime and why the announcement of it can go hand in hand with the demonization of religion: you are free to express your religious views, not because of their content, but because of their status as expression. Religious views in this understanding are just like other views – political views, aesthetic views, sexual views, baseball views – and what is valued about them is that they have been freely produced – no one forced you to utter them – and that they are freely broadcast – no one has censored them. What is *not* valued about them is what they urge. As instances of a favoured category – expression – religious utterances are cherished; as something to take seriously, they are feared and condemned.

I have lingered over the example of religion because it can stand for what liberalism, in the name of academic freedom, does to any form of strong conviction that refuses to respect (or even recognize) the line between the private and the public, between the cerebral and the political, and that moves instead to institutionalize itself in the rule of law. The "Trent University Statement on Free Inquiry and Expression" claims that "academic freedom makes commitment possible." No, it makes commitment, except to expression, suspect, or rather, it makes possible and *mandates* commitment to academic freedom, which requires as the price for being able to proclaim your views that you tolerate the views of others, even those "you do not condone and, in some cases, deplore."[8]

Now it is hard to know exactly what "deplore" means in such a statement. For the ethic of tolerance to make sense, "deplore" must indicate a revulsion that is merely personal, as in "I deplore the ties he wears" or "I deplore the music she listens to." Deploring something on that level does not involve the determination to stamp it out, root and branch. If, however, by "deplore" you mean "fear" or "think dangerous" or "find evil," then it is not clear why you would be so willing to allow what you deplore to flourish. Academic freedom is coherent only if you assume that the things you freely allow will be innocuous and containable, which they will be if they are regarded not as calls to action but as material for discussion, preferably in the setting of a seminar. If, however, a form of speech or advocacy will not offer itself as material for discussion but simply declares itself to be the *truth* to which all must bend, academic freedom will reject it as illiberal, just as it rejects religious speech seriously urged.

What this means is that academic freedom, rather than being "open to all points of view," is open to all points of view *only* so long as they offer themselves with the reserve and diffidence appropriate to Enlightenment decorums and only so long as they offer themselves for correction. In short, academic freedom places severe limits on what can go on in its playground, and it is in fact a form of closure. Academic freedom is not a defence against orthodoxy; it *is* an orthodoxy and a faith: the orthodoxy is rational deliberation, and the faith – somewhat paradoxically – is that through rational deliberation we shall arrive at the truth of whose existence rational deliberation is so sceptical.

To say that academic freedom is an orthodoxy is not to score a fatal point against it. Even if academic freedom is deprived of the claim to be hostage to no single point of view, it survives as a point of view you might reasonably want to embrace; and the question to put to it, *as* point of view, is what does it urge and what does it exclude? The answer to that question has already been partly given by the example of religion. Academic freedom urges the interrogation of all propositions and the privileging of none, the equal right of all voices to be heard, no matter how radical or unsettling, and the obligation to subject even one's most cherished convictions to the scrutiny of reason. What academic freedom excludes is any position that refuses that obligation – any position that rests on pronouncements such as "I am the way" or "Thou shalt have no other gods before me."

To be sure, a champion of academic freedom would say that those positions are not excluded at all; rather, they are invited into the seminar, where they can be discussed, interrogated, reasoned with, analyzed. But of course, that is not what the proponents of doctrinaire agendas want; they want to win; they want to occupy and be sovereign over the discursive space and to expel others from it, and this position is what academic freedom will not permit. (It wants to win, too, and *does* by exiling from its confines any discourse that violates its rules.) In short, academic freedom invites forceful agendas in, but only on *its* terms, and refuses to grant legitimacy to the terms within which such agendas define themselves. We are right back to the 1915 AAUP declaration with a slight modification: religion can be part of university life so long as it renounces its claim to have a privileged purchase on the truth, which is the claim that defines a religion as a religion as opposed to a mere opinion.

It's a great move whereby liberalism, in the form of academic freedom, gets to display its generosity while at the same time cutting the heart out of the views to which that generosity is extended. It is not only a great move, it is also a move that works, in part because it comes packaged in a vocabulary of rights that is also a theory of personhood. In that theory, you are defined as the bearer of rights (the right to believe, the right to speak, the right to choose) and not by the content of the acts you perform when exercising them. From this definition of personhood follows what I called at the beginning of this chapter the logic of reciprocal rights, for if what makes you what you are is your capacity for speech, belief, and choice and not what you believe, say, or choose, then you are obligated, as a mark of self-respect, to respect the beliefs, utterances, and choices of others, because they are incidental to the essence you and those others share. If your neighbours' meat is your poison, then you should just refrain from eating it while leaving them to eat what they like; if your colleagues' positions on abortion or affirmative action are anathema to you, debate them while upholding their right to have them so long as they uphold your right to have yours. What is sauce for the goose is sauce for the gander.

It all sounds fine and highly moral, but in fact it displaces morality by asking you to inhabit your moral convictions loosely and be ready to withdraw from them when pursuing them would impinge on the activities and choices of others. In short, the what's sauce for the goose is sauce for the gander argument asks you to be morally thin by asking you to conceive of yourself not as someone who is committed to something but as someone who is committed to respecting the commitments of those with whom he or she disagrees. Again, this argument sounds fine until you realize that it requires you to suspend those very urgencies that move you to act in the world and to regard them as no different from the urgencies of your enemies. To put the matter from the other direction: the logic of what's sauce for the goose is sauce for the gander requires that you redescribe your enemy as someone just like you. Indeed, in this vision, there are no enemies (except religious zealots), just persons with different preferences, and if that's all there is, you certainly don't want to silence, or penalize, or even imprison people just because they don't share your preferences. Again, for the third time, this argument sounds fine *if* you don't detect the sleight of hand involved whereby convictions and life allegiances are turned into preferences, much as free speech doctrine turns all utterances into opinions. In this profoundly reductive scenario, everything is like everything else, neither something to live for nor something to fight for. Once moral stances have been turned into individual preferences and assertions into opinions, it makes perfect sense that you refrain from acting on them in ways that would interfere with the freedom of others to prefer differently. I think the Holocaust really happened; you think it didn't; let's agree to disagree, that's what makes horse races, and who is to judge anyway? Any tendency to judge and to enforce your judgment by an act of coercion will be met by someone asking, "How would you like it if someone did that to you?" – a question that assumes that you and the hypothetical someone are interchangeable, exactly alike except for a few moral, political, or religious views; and that the act you wouldn't want done to you is abstract, identifiable apart from any set of circumstances or motives, and a violation of right no matter who does it to whom.

The result is not only a self rendered morally thin but a society rendered morally thin when the logic of reciprocal rights is invoked to forbid the state from taking any action that endorses or seems to endorse one point of view over another. In a landmark case (*American Booksellers v. Hudnut*), the US Appeals Court for the seventh circuit struck down an antipornography ordinance because it enshrined in law a particular view of women – the view that they are human beings and not sex objects – rather than the alternative view found in pornography. The same withdrawal from moral judgment and from morality – on the basis, supposedly, of principle – is the content of the phrase "reverse racism" – the idea that any action taken on the basis of a racial classification is equivalent to any other action taken on the basis of racial classification. Justice Clarence Thomas had the move down pat when he declared in *Adarand* v. *Pena* (512 U.S. 200, [1995]) that "it is irrelevant whether ... racial classifications are drawn by those who wish to oppress a race or by those who have a sincere desire to help the previously oppressed. In each instance, it is racial discrimination plain and simple." But the word "irrelevant" should alert us to the cost of the plainness and simplicity Thomas so confidently announces: We must discount – declare irrelevant – the moral and historical difference between the oppressed and the oppressor. Supreme Court Justice Stevens on his part, is unwilling to do so, and he answers Thomas with his own plain and simple point: "There is no moral or constitutional equivalence between a policy ... designed to perpetrate a caste system and one that seeks to eradicate racial subordination." Of course, these practices can be *made* equivalent if you first detach them from the real-world purposes that made them what they were in the first place and then recharacterize them as interchangeable instances of a conceptual category, such as the category of "race consciousness," which Thomas declares to be odious and inherently suspect, no matter what the intentions and practices of those who display it. Armed with this scalpel, you can find Ku Klux Klan lynchings no different from efforts to deny the Klan representation in public spaces; you can find the exclusion for centuries of minorities from the construction industry no different from minority set-aside programs; you can find quotas designed to exclude races from institutions of higher education no different from admissions procedures that take race into account; you can find that the Voting Rights Act, passed to grant blacks a share of the franchise, can be invoked by whites who declare themselves disenfranchised by that act; you can find the rantings of neo-Nazis no different from – indeed, more legitimate than – the proclamation of the golden rule, on the reasoning, first, that they are both expressions and, second, that the golden rule is an expression of a religious viewpoint and therefore out of bounds in a forum dedicated to academic freedom.

This is where liberal neutrality, academic freedom, and the principle of what's sauce for the goose is sauce for the gander get you: to a forced inability to make distinctions that would be perspicuous to any well-informed teenager – distinctions between lynchings and set-asides, between a Shakespearean sonnet and hard-core pornography, between, in Justice Steven's words, a welcome mat and a no-entry sign. It is an inability that follows from shifting situations out of the historical context that gave them meaning and into an abstract context where they have no meaning. Here is another example. Samuel Walker, writing as a member of the American Civil Liberties Union – that curious organization whose mission it is to find things it hates and then grow them – complains because at different times the Supreme Court of the United States protected the National Association for the Advancement of Colored People from acts of harassment but declined to protect the Ku Klux Klan from similar acts. The only difference, says Walker, is the "reputation of the organization under attack."[9] Right. The only difference is the difference between the Klan and the NAACP, and if that's not a difference, then I don't know what is. In 1959, Columbia Law School professor Herbert Wechsler declared himself unable to justify the desegregation decision *Brown* v. *Board of Education*[10] because as far as he could see, the choice the case offered was between the wish of blacks freely to associate and the wish of whites freely not to associate. Wechsler reports he can find no principle that favours one wish over the other. But Wechsler's dilemma is of his own making; it follows from his having turned the richly contextualized actions of agents embedded in particular histories with particular agendas into abstract wishes with no content except the desire to prevail. It is only when these wishes float free of everything that animated them in the first place that they will seem indistinguishable and incapable of being sorted out, even by a famous law professor.

The question is, why would anyone *reason* as Wechsler and Thomas and the seventh circuit court do? And the answer is, because reasoning *that* way has a payoff in outcomes *someone* desires: the rollback of affirmative action, the perpetuation of male dominance, the flourishing of arguments for racial superiority. The way of thinking that produces an inability to make otherwise obvious distinctions is not politically innocent; it is a political weapon wielded self-consciously, and often skilfully, by persons and groups with definite goals in mind. Those goals are *not* free speech, open inquiry, mutual respect, and so on, but sales of pornography, maintenance of lily-white construction crews, the disadvantaging of minority religions, and so on. If liberal neutrality cannot make good on its claim to be above the fray (and it certainly cannot), then it is necessarily embroiled in the fray, coming down on one side rather than another, and doing so with an effectiveness that is inversely proportional to the plausibility of the claim it cannot make good on. Liberal neutrality does political work so well because it has managed to assume the mantle of being above political work, and if you don't like the political work it is doing, you must labour to take the mantle away, strip off the veneer of principle so that policies wearing the mask of principle will be forced to identify themselves for what they are and for what they are not.

In your efforts to do so, the vocabulary and rhetoric of multiculturalism will not help. I said at the outset that I may have found a position no one likes. Liberal defenders of academic freedom won't like it, but neither should defenders of multiculturalism, if only because they are liberal defenders of academic freedom in slightly different clothing. Whereas the watchwords of liberal defenders of academic freedom are neutrality and impartiality, the watchwords of multiculturalists are difference and diversity; but just as neutrality and impartiality mandate the exclusion of strong religious views from their circle, so do difference and diversity mandate the exclusion of views alleging racial superiority or the immorality of homosexuals. Liberal neutrality and multiculturalism are both engines of exclusion trying to fly under inclusive banners.

That is why people on the wrong side of these respective engines feel suffocated when they get going, why minorities protest that neutrality is a sham, and middle-aged white professors, like me, protest that diversity reaches out to include everyone but them. Both sides are right. They *are* being excluded. Where they are wrong is in thinking that *in*clusion, of a truly capacious kind, is possible. All that is possible – all you can work for – is to arrange things so that the inevitable exclusions are favourable to your interests and hostile to the interests of your adversaries. The inclusive university is not an attainable goal. It is not even a worthy one, for to attain it would be to legitimize all points of view and directions of inquiry, defaulting on the responsibility of the university to produce knowledge and to refine judgment. The debate is never between the inclusive university and the university marked by exclusions; the debate is always between competing structures of exclusion; and the debate ends, at least for a time, when one structure of exclusion manages to make its interests perfectly congruent with what is understood by the term "academic freedom." The assertion of interest is always what's going on – even when, and especially when, interest wraps itself in high-sounding abstractions.

This is not an indictment of anyone and certainly not an indictment of anyone for having forsaken principles for politics; politics is all there is, and it's a good thing too. Principles and abstractions don't exist except as the rhetorical accompaniments of practices in search of good public relations. This is not an indictment either, just an observation and perhaps advice. Be alert to those moments when your opponents have a public relations machine so good that it's killing you; for then, you're going to have to stop and try to take it apart. Right now, the public relations machine that rides on the tracks of the ethic of mutual respect and the mantra of academic freedom is in such high gear that those whose interests are likely to be rolled over by it had better do something. That's what I have been trying to do here by explaining, over and over again, how these formulas work, the kind of work they do, and why, if you look beneath them, you may not like what you see. I am not so naive as to believe that I have persuaded you, but I will be more than pleased if when you next hear someone say what is sauce for the goose is sauce for the gander, or you are tempted to say it yourself, you at least hesitate – and remember that a goose *is* a goose and not a gander – before surrendering to the satisfaction of liberal complacency.

**Notes**

Some of the material in this chapter was published previously in *The Trouble with Principle* (Cambridge, MA: Harvard University Press), 35-45.

1 Immanuel Kant, *Political Writings*, ed. Hans S. Reiss (Cambridge: Cambridge University Press, 1991), 74.

2 John Stuart Mill, "On Liberty," in *Texts: Commentaries*, ed. Alan Ryan (London: Norton, 1997), 108.

3 *Freedom and Tenure in the Academy*, ed. W.W. Van Alstyne (Durham: Duke University Press, 1993), 394.

4 Walter Metzger, "The 1940 Statement of Principle on Academic Freedom and Tenure," in *Freedom and Tenure in the Academy*, ed. W.W. Van Alstyne (Durham: Duke University Press, 1993), 36.

5 John Fekete, *Moral Panic: Biopolitics Rising* (Montreal: Robert Davies, 1995), 200, 203.

6 Ronald Dworkin, "We Need a New Interpretation of Academic Freedom," in *The Future of Academic Freedom*, ed. Louis Menand (Chicago: University of Chicago Press, 1996), 189.

7   *Reynolds* v. *United States* (1878), in *First Amendment Cases and Materials*, ed. W.W. Van Alstyne (Westbury, NY: Foundation Press, 1991), 932.
8   Fekete.
9   Samuel Walker, *Hate Speech* (London: University of Nebraska Press, 1994), 27.
10  Herbert Wechsler, "Toward Neutral Principles of Constitutional Law," *Harvard Law Review* 73 (1959): 1-35.

# 2
# Academic Freedom: Rights as Immunities and Privileges
*Frederick Schauer*

Like most academics, I am not the world's most politically or socially astute person. Nevertheless, I am astute enough not to take a position on a heated, political controversy about which I know little and in a country that is not my own. If you were to ask me what I do, I would say that I engage in conceptual clarification. Consequently, I believe it is important we get things straight before we can get them right. Moreover, I believe it is important to help people subject their own ideas to rigorous testing, because such testing is the beginning, the middle, and the end of intellectual honesty. Such testing is what I shall attempt here.

It has been astutely suggested that things appearing in opposition, like inclusiveness and academic freedom, may not necessarily be in opposition, and at such times, conceptual reconfiguration may help us. I think that is often right. Conceptual reconfiguration, however, may make it harder to recognize the opposition that frequently does exist and that should not be defined or assumed away.

Accordingly, I want to explore whether the tension or opposition between the goals we think of as inclusiveness and academic freedom are real. And part of what I hope to explain is what I and many other Americans think of as academic freedom, leaving open the question of whether any other country, or my country for that matter, would want to have such a thing.

Rather than defining academic freedom so that nobody could deny its virtues, I want to define it more crisply and make it possible to debate the question of whether it is in fact a good thing, which I consider an open question. I take my guide from the turn-of-the-century American legal philosopher, now somewhat more influential outside the United States than in, Wesley Newcombe Hohfeld. In talking about and analyzing rights, Hohfeld recognized that many things often went under the name of rights that were quite different from each other. He thought it important to separate different conceptions and structures of rights, and relationships between rights.

One of those structures was what he called a privilege and what others called an immunity. This kind of right is most relevant to the question of academic freedom. Let me be clearer. When I talk about an immunity or a privilege, I am largely talking about an exemption from something that everyone else has to do. A certain kind of right, a certain kind of privilege, fits this categorization because there is a general obligation from which some people are exempted. In the context of military conscription, conscientious objector status is one good example. In the law of evidence, the privilege of a spouse not to testify against his or her spouse is another. Other examples include the privileges between priest and penitent, doctor and patient, and lawyer and client, or the privilege that journalists claim, and in some countries are given, not to disclose their sources. For all these privileges, there is a corresponding general, social obligation, whether it be an obligation to conscription, to testify in court, or to disclose information relevant to a crime. And the status of certain people sometimes grants them an exemption from this otherwise "universal" social, legal, or political requirement. Such is the issue when we think about academic freedom. Then the question is whether certain people or certain institutions, because of their status and the roles they perform, ought to get this exemption from what everyone else has to do.

Academic freedom debates always seem to me to fit this characterization, although their status may vary dramatically from country to country. For example, there are now active debates about academic freedom in South Africa. But in South Africa, the debates are not so much about the prerogatives of individual faculty members, or the prerogatives of departments, or the prerogatives of disciplines, as they are about the universities' autonomy from general political control; that is, in South Africa, the debate is about whether universities should be viewed as other bureaucracies and other departments in a parliamentary system and, therefore, subject to the directives of parliamentary authority. The argument about academic freedom is whether universities, as universities, regardless of what they may do internally, ought to be given greater autonomy from external political control than that given to other government departments. This argument is a somewhat different form of debate than we most commonly see in North America, but it is still a form of debate in which there is claim for an exemption or immunity from what would otherwise be the general or prevailing principle.

Once we think about academic freedom as an exemption or immunity, we realize that what we are thinking about switches the burden of the argument in a way that might help us think more clearly about the difficulty in many of the most common claims about academic freedom. Consider American experience on this issue. As a form of discourse, academic freedom became prominent in the United States in the 1950s and 1960s, during and in the wake of McCarthyism: at various times, the Supreme Court of the United

States, in protecting the free speech and free association rights of people employed by universities, referred to the overriding importance of academic freedom. The concept came up in the context of loyalty oaths, in the context of memberships in various organizations, and in the context of various speeches that people might have given outside their classroom or outside their employment, in the narrowest sense of that employment. Yet, despite the fact that American law in the 1950s and 1960s contained all this grandiloquent language about academic freedom, it was generally makeweight and had no legal implications whatsoever.

Let me explain with two contrasting examples. Think about a university professor who is a member of the Communist Party. The Supreme Court of the United States said in the late 1950s and 1960s that a faculty member employed by a state university, and thus by a governmental institution, could not be dismissed from that position for being a member of the Communist Party and for taking political positions consistent with those of the Communist Party. The court talked about this situation in the standard American free speech language with which you are probably familiar. Yet at the same time the Supreme Court was also making roughly the same point about other government employees who did not happen to be university professors. It was saying the same thing about sanitation workers, construction workers, bureaucrats, and the like, and thus the principle turned out to be not about academic freedom but rather about the principle that employees of the government, including but not limited to university professors, could not be dismissed for exercising the free speech and free association rights held by all other citizens. Although issues of academic freedom were lingering when this issue came up in the university, the issue was not really academic freedom. The issue was not about an exemption or an immunity. It was simply about principles that would apply to everyone and, therefore, did not concern the question of whether university people ought to get an exemption from what was required of others.

So, the issue of whether academics should get exemptions from what is required of other citizens rarely comes up in the United States, although occasionally it does in the context of immunities not related to speaking or writing. For example, the Supreme Court a few years ago dealt with a claim that in affirmative action and discrimination investigations, academic institutions were privileged to keep secret their internal processes, even though other organizations did not. The court easily rejected this claim and, in effect, said that an institution was not exempt from all of the enforcement mechanisms of the discrimination laws just because it claimed to be an academic institution or university. More commonly, in many places in the world, this issue might come up in the context of exemptions for academics from what would otherwise be restrictions on freedom of speech. It turns out this situation is not much of an issue in the United States, because although academic freedom might not be an issue, the United States – if you will allow me a bit of hyperbole – protects everything, controversially and, in my view, often wrongly. And given that everything is protected, there isn't much room to claim that things that are not protected for general citizens ought to be protected for academics.

Let me give a more concrete example in the context of a noticeable contrast between the United States and Canada. Consider the issue of holocaust denial. In the United States, holocaust denial is fully protected by the First Amendment, in ways that the *Keegstra, Zündell, Andrews,* and *Taylor* cases make clear that in Canada it is often not protected. In many contexts, denying the Holocaust in Canada is an offence; in the United States, it is not. In Canada, then, an academic freedom claim would assert that something not generally protected – the right to deny the existence of the Holocaust in public communication – would become protected when done by an academic, precisely because of the features of academic life that academics claim justify the special immunity or special privilege of academic freedom. But because in the United States everybody has this right, the issue does not come up. So, one way of characterizing this strand of academic freedom in the context of the United States, in the specific context of an exemption from what otherwise would be the constitutionally permissible restrictions on speech for citizens, might be to say that there is no academic freedom in the United States, but that does not matter. On this issue, there is no exemption: Why would anybody want or need one, given the prevailing principles? In countries, including Canada and every other country on the face of the earth that is not the United States, restrictions on speech in the name of inclusiveness, antiracism, equality, and the like are deemed more acceptable.

I might point out that the 1965 International Convention on the Elimination of All Forms of Discrimination requires its signatory nations to have laws prohibiting the incitement to racial hatred. The United States has refused to join this part of the convention precisely because the laws necessary in the service of an international convention and international conceptions of equality would be patently unconstitutional under American constitutional doctrine. I could go on to talk somewhat critically and sceptically about my own country's laws in this regard, but that is a different topic; I only use this example to show why it may be a mistake to look south for guidance on issues of freedom and speech.

Another way of clarifying the question, but one still consistent with the idea of a privileged exemption or immunity, would be to think of an exemption or immunity from what would otherwise be the prevailing principles of supervisory authority within a university. Now we are getting somewhat closer to a crisper conception of an academic freedom immunity. In most contexts, those who work in positions in which they are subject to supervision are expected to follow the instructions and orders of their supervisors. This expectation applies to the full range of people who might work in state employment. It certainly does so in the United States. In that sense, although we can talk about academic freedom as an immunity, we would not in the United States talk about employee freedom; that is, in general, there is no constitutional right for state employees to disregard the instructions or orders of their employers.

Let us think about professionals in general. Let us say we have a dentist working for the government. The dental authority tells the dentist how to clean or fill or drill, and the dentist claims these detailed instructions interfere with professional autonomy. After all, the dentist is a professional who went to dental school and has a right to exercise autonomy. That all makes a lot of sense, but it does not rise to the level of a constitutional right. What we would say to the dentist is "We sympathize with your plight, but you have no legal, constitutional, or even moral claim." The right to professional autonomy does not rise to the level of a legal or constitutional exemption from principles of supervisory prerogative.

It is in this context that university academics claim something in the name of academic freedom that looks like what dentists are claiming. But academics are claiming something that dentists do not get by virtue of dentistry and that academics claim by virtue of being academics: an exemption from otherwise applicable supervisory obligations. Let me give an example. Consider first the classroom. When I was at the University of Michigan, I was a state employee. One of my supervisors was Harold Shapiro, who at the time was president of the university. Imagine the following scenario. Suppose that President Shapiro said to me, "I hear that in your courses in American constitutional law you are teaching a sceptical view of the American free speech tradition. I am your supervisor, you are my subordinate, and I want you to teach differently." In the United States, I would then claim an exemption from otherwise applicable principles of responsibility to my superior. And American law on this subject would support my claim.

What is interesting is that on the issue, American law distinguishes primary and secondary schools from universities. Let us make it more controversial. Suppose in teaching about equality under the Fourteenth Amendment, I said I believe equality is not a particularly good idea; that the problem with the modern world is that we have too much equality and not too little of it; and that the Fourteenth Amendment was a bad idea. Again, I could not be dismissed for that. My academic freedom claims of exemption from what would otherwise be applicable requirements would prevail. But if the same thing had come up in the case of a primary or secondary school teacher who wanted to teach that equality was a bad thing, the claims would lose.

In the United States, we distinguish universities from primary and secondary schools on the theory that in universities there ought to be freedom to be a social critic. I want to put it somewhat more strongly. In the United States, we believe that academic institutions ought to be havens for heresy, ought to be the kind of place where things can be said or thought or written that would otherwise be unthinkable. That may or may not be a good idea, but it is no mere matter of style: when it is most controversial, it turns out to be a matter of substance. And when it is most controversial, it makes the classroom a less equal, less comfortable, and less inclusive place. For example, a discussion of the heritability of intelligence will make some students in class uncomfortable and therefore less able to participate in that learning environment.

When we think about heresy or being social critics, think about a university professor who teaches that inclusiveness is a bad idea. By the very virtue of its saying, this idea makes the classroom and the university less inclusive. Most American children at about the age of seven come running home from the playground saying, "Johnny just called me a such-and-such." Then our parents say to us, "Don't worry about it. Sticks and stones may break your bones, but names will never hurt you." By the time we are nine years old, we realize that this assurance is false. Words make a difference, language makes a difference, and an academic who in the service of being a social critic, in the service of challenging the unchallengeable, and in the service of being a member of the department of heresy, challenges inclusiveness, taking on prevailing views about issues of equality and in effect making the learning environment less inclusive and less equal. Conversely, if in the service of the goals of inclusiveness, issues of inclusiveness, equality, discrimination, diversity, and multiculturalism ought not be talked about in ways that make students less able to enjoy the benefits of the university, then some people will find it harder to challenge fundamental social ideas.

This crux can be thought of as a question of decision theory. Those of you who have endured a basic course in statistics may be familiar with the distinction between Type I and Type II errors. The Type I error here is the nonarticulation of an idea that might turn out to be true. The Type II error here is the articulation of a false idea that does harm because of its falsity. If we are worried about Type II errors and minimize them, we increase the number of Type I errors. If we are worried about the Type I errors and minimize them, we increase the number of Type II errors. Thus, I want to reemphasize this issue of unavoidability. If we focus on the unavoidable, we may recognize that the issues are harder than we thought they were. But as I have said, academics ought not try to avoid the hard issues. Rather, I want people to be as hard on their own ideas as they can be.

Now, finally, if we think of the rights of both sides of the issue in rights-based terms, we may arrive at a different picture of rights. There is a picture of rights that is widely rampant in all parts of North America: rights are what keep bad people from doing bad things. They guard us against dictators; they guard us against pirates. Under this picture of rights, protecting rights prevents bad people from doing bad things and therefore incurs no social cost. A more challenging and more realistic picture of rights is that rights are side constraints, to use philosophical terminology, on short- and intermediate-term welfare maximization. Thus considered, rights keep good people from doing good things, and rights do so in the service of long term objectives or in the service of nonconsequentialist objectives. If rights are, at times, the things that keep good people from doing good things, and do so in the service of long-term objectives (for example, they keep good people from restricting harmful speech or keep good people from restricting harmful, dangerous, and wrong academics), then it turns out that protecting rights is no longer free of social cost. If protecting rights is no longer free, the debate about which rights we should have and when we should have them becomes much more difficult, but that, at least for an academic, is no excuse for avoiding the debate.

# 3
# What's at Stake?
# Intersections and Tensions
*Lynn Smith*

"What is at stake?" I shall address this question indirectly through some speculations about why this debate is often difficult and emotional. Next, I shall argue that if the new norms of equality are to be implemented, they will require some reshaping of concepts, including the concept of academic freedom. Finally, I shall suggest that when the goals of academic freedom and inclusivity are understood in light of one another, they are not necessarily inconsistent.

I will take a brief detour to clarify how the Canadian Charter of Rights and Freedoms applies to universities. It has been suggested from time to time that within the university there is a lesser right to freedom of expression or other Charter rights than exists outside the university. In my view, that is not the case. The Charter applies to legislatures and governments. The Supreme Court of Canada has said that the universities are not governments or branches of government and, accordingly, that the universities *as such* are not bound by the Charter (though they are bound by human rights and employment legislation). Nevertheless, the university is not a Charter-free zone. Everyone within the university has the same Charter rights as all other citizens. Constraints on the activities of the police and other agents of the government apply on campuses as they do everywhere else. Constraints on legislative activity affecting the university apply as they do to all legislative activity. Thus, for example, if amendments to the Universities Act infringe the Charter, they can be challenged in court. Similarly, if arrests or searches on campus infringe the Charter, they also can be challenged. Beyond these ways in which the Charter affects universities, the values embodied in the Charter and the interpretive principles that courts have enunciated flowing from those values have a tendency to infuse discussion and to guide decision making even where the Charter does not directly apply, as in the development of harassment policies or in the resolution of academic freedom disputes.

Disputes about academic freedom and inclusiveness share a common feature: an attempt to make faculty members accountable to students or colleagues. What is at stake, then, when there is an imposition of accountability is the loss of the state of *not* being accountable or of not *feeling* accountable – a delightful state to be sure, and one whose loss understandably is feared by those who enjoy it. What is also at stake is the attainment of the state of being truly and meaningfully included – a state much to be desired as well. I won't suggest that the reconciliation is easy, but I will suggest that it is possible in principle and in practice.

Having tried to suggest something of what is at stake, I will identify some of the underlying tensions by asking the question "Why is this debate so difficult?"

First, the historical origins of the universities still have a role in shaping them. In thirteenth-century universities, there were several founding faculties: law, medicine, theology, and arts. But there was only one founding gender: male. The epigraph of David Noble's *A World without Women: The Christian Clerical Culture of Western Science*[1] is a quotation from Johannes Scotus Erigena: "At the Resurrection, sex will be abolished and nature made one ... There will then be only man, as if he had never sinned." According to Noble, by the high Middle Ages the clerical ascetic culture of the Latin church hierarchy (reflected in the words of John Scotus) had become the culture of the entire priesthood and the culture of learning. The shift to include females in the university is of recent origin. It is not surprising that the effects are still being felt. Similarly, the adoption of diversity policies and the opening of doors to Aboriginal peoples, members of racial minorities, and persons with disabilities are even more recent. It takes time to work out the consequences of such significant shifts.

Corresponding with and to some extent causing the opening of the doors to the university is the very recent shift in the stated (official) norms about participation in Canadian society. There are now authoritative statements in law and public policy (for example, in human rights legislation) that men and women, all races, all ethnic backgrounds, religions, ages, and levels of physical or mental ability are entitled to equality and to freedom from discrimination. The Canadian Charter of Rights and Freedoms not only creates constitutional protection for the fundamental freedoms, including freedom of expression, but also establishes constitutional equality rights. With respect to both the freedom of expression and the equality rights, the influence of these constitutional statements extends well beyond the limits of formal application of the Charter. It will take time to work through the implications of the profound shift in our paradigm of equality. This is because it is not just a question of removing formal barriers. These laws say not only that formal exclusion should be eliminated but also that gender, race, ethnicity, religion, disability, and the like should be accommodated in public institutions – and that so far as possible those factors should not limit access to those institutions.

Another reason why this discussion is difficult flows from the tendency to view the American situation as the default position or norm. In the case of the constitutional equality guarantees, the Canadian courts have broken new ground and taken a substantive, not merely a formal, approach to equality. This substantive approach to equality means the question is not whether similarly situated people are treated similarly but whether historically disadvantaged groups face a lack of equality in their political, social, or economic position. For example, the earlier position was that discrimination in the workplace based on pregnancy is not sex discrimination so long as all pregnant persons are treated alike. The current constitutional position is that it is sex discrimination because of its effect of heightening the disadvantage of women. As well, Canadian courts have departed from the implicit American norm in saying that the Charter does not stipulate a hierarchy of rights – no single right trumps the other. Freedom of expression and equality are parallel; both are to be read with an understanding of the other.

The protection for academic freedom is almost as new as the equality guarantees. The achievement of academic freedom basically occurred in the twentieth century. Not only is it a recent development, but much of the working out of the implications has taken place during a period influenced by the "romantic ideal of scholarship," emphasizing personal creativity, which is seen to permit no restraints.[2] This romantic ideal of scholarship tends to take an absolutist view of what is required for academic freedom. (Perhaps as a corollary, or perhaps independently, academics occasionally provide empirical basis for Stanley Fish's claim about the academic psyche. He speaks of the "remarkable uniform incompetence of academic administrators."[3] Saying that academics "get the administrators that they want," he adds: "By getting the administrators they want, academics get what they *really* want – they get to be downtrodden; and by getting to be downtrodden, academics get what they really *really* want – they get to complain ... The reason that academics want and need their complaints is that it is important to them to feel oppressed, for in the psychic economy of the academy, oppression is the sign of virtue."[4]) A related observation is that within the employment relationship, faculty members are individual professionals who do their work without any particular oversight or direction as to how they do it. Discussions of accountability and oversight in the context of harassment or discrimination issues are therefore somewhat novel. This fact means not only that legitimate grievances may be overlooked or trivialized but also that trivial grievances may be taken very seriously and waste a great deal of time. With more experience, a sense of judgment and confidence in dealing with these matters develops.

My next point concerns the reshaping of concepts. As a result of the statement of new norms of equality, a reshaping of concepts is under way in many public and private institutions. Examples are the concept of the family and the concept of liberty. With respect to the latter, Madam Justice Bertha Wilson points out in her reasons in *Morgentaler* (in which the Supreme Court of Canada struck down the Criminal Code prohibition against abortion)[5] that the concept of liberty was developed in the context of state intrusions on citizens – then defined as male – who wished to do the kinds of things that male citizens did at the time the concept emerged: they wanted to speak their minds, they wanted to join groups, they did not want to be arbitrarily arrested or detained, and so on. Madam Justice Wilson says that we now must understand liberty in a way that makes it fully meaningful for both men and women; that we must envision the right holder as a woman (indeed, as a pregnant woman). What would "liberty" mean if pregnant women had participated in the development of the concept? Madam Justice Wilson's view is correct: that "liberty" would include the right to make decisions about whether to terminate pregnancies.

Academic freedom and the inclusive university are being reshaped. Having stated a new set of norms about equality in Canadian society, we have created expectations – appropriate expectations – that universities will be places where people will be treated with equal concern and respect when they become members of that community; that is, we have created expectations that universities will be inclusive. When these expectations are not met, people will complain, sometimes wrongly, sometimes overly strongly, but often justifiably. In my view, academic freedom has never meant and cannot mean that academics are free from all criticism, challenge, or accountability. Challenges to curriculum and pedagogy may be a nuisance, but the fact that they must be addressed is perfectly consistent with academic freedom. Debate, even when relevant and properly conducted, about race, gender, or other similar issues might make some participants uncomfortable. However, although discomfort may be unavoidable, a competent instructor can present material and conduct discussion in a manner that does not create a sense of exclusion or intimidation.

My third and final point is that academic freedom and inclusivity are not necessarily inconsistent. I am going to refer to one particular formulation of this argument by University of Toronto philosopher Fred Wilson, though similar arguments have been made by others. His point is that academic freedom is not an unconditional right. It brings obligations. It is conferred by contract and is not a natural law or a basic human right. It is an instrumental creation intended to achieve certain purposes; namely, as Wilson says, "Academic freedom is granted in order that truth actually be sought in teaching and research: in return for being able to pursue truth fearlessly, professors must accept the obligation to pursue the truth."[6] As the Canadian

Association of University Teachers (CAUT) "Policy Statement on Academic Freedom" puts it, "Academic freedom carries with it 'the duty to use that freedom in a manner consistent with the scholarly obligation to base research and teaching on an honest search for knowledge.'"[7] It is inconsistent with an honest search for knowledge to illegitimately marginalize or to exclude persons or points of view; that is, irrationally and without fair consideration for what they have to say. It is inconsistent with an honest search for knowledge to brook no criticism; to fail to conduct classes so that students feel free to say that they wonder why the curriculum does not include something or that they would prefer to be addressed in one manner rather than another. In particular, as Wilson says, "There is the obligation to engage in the discourse of the academy."[8] Academic freedom is the freedom to participate without fear in that discourse. The obligations to teach and conduct research in the university are requirements to participate in that discourse. These obligations are to engage in rational debate with one's colleagues engaged in research and with one's students in the classroom. Professors are not to treat the classroom as a pulpit, a place for the inculcation of dogma rather than a place for rational debate. They must not illegitimately exclude from that rational discourse other members, and aspiring members, of the academy. The right to academic freedom ensures that others will not interfere with one's own participation in that discourse. At least, so one hopes. It is not always so, however, and that is why we need, as the CAUT makes clear, settled procedures for resolving complaints and grievances in this area – procedures that conform to the requirements of fairness and natural justice. As Amy Gutmann writes: "Multicultural societies and communities that stand for the freedom and equality of all people rest upon mutual respect for reasonable intellectual, political, and cultural differences. Mutual respect requires a widespread willingness and ability to articulate our disagreements, to defend them before people with whom we disagree, to discern the difference between respectable and disrespectable disagreement, and to be open to changing our own minds when faced with well-reasoned criticism. The moral promise of multiculturalism depends on the exercise of these deliberative virtues."[9]

Academic freedom can continue to be robustly protected while equality becomes robustly promoted. Should academic freedom take priority over subjective discomfort? Yes. Should promotion of equality take priority over unfettered expression of whatever may occur to an individual scholar, even when irrelevant to the subject matter, simply because it flows from his or her personal creativity? Yes. Will there be difficult, disputatious cases that don't fall clearly on one side of the line or the other? Yes. To resolve them, an understanding of *why* we protect academic freedom and *why* we promote equality will provide guiding principles.

## Notes

1  David Noble, *A World without Women: The Christian Clerical Culture of Western Science* (New York and Toronto: Alfred A. Knopf, 1992), vii.
2  Fred Wilson, " In Defence of Speech Codes," *Interchange* 27 (1996): 150.
3  Stanley Fish, *There's No Such Thing as Free Speech ... And It's a Good Thing, Too* (New York: Oxford University Press, 1994): 276.
4  Fish, 276.
5  *R. v. Morgentaler*, [1988] 1 SCR 30.
6  Wilson, 131.
7  Wilson, quoting CAUT "Policy Statement on Academic Freedom."
8  Wilson, 137.
9  Amy Gutmann, introduction to *Multiculturalism and "The Politics of Recognition,"* by Charles Taylor (Princeton: Princeton University Press, 1992), 23-4.

# Part 2
# The Changing Culture

# 4
# The Role of Universities in a Changing Culture
*Bernard Shapiro*

Our cultural, political, and economic environments shift with such speed that even the most acute observers have difficulty bringing things into focus. How then can one accurately consider the future role of universities?

Universities exist to serve the society that supports them, but in what way and with what type of educational and scholarly commitment? The answers to these questions depend in large part on society's aspirations and the challenges it faces. It is difficult, however, to know which of the many developing and sometimes conflicting motifs we see about us will become the dominant themes of the future. New challenges to the human condition are emerging, including demography, different forms of communication, the environment, technology, and political and cultural fragmentation (if not disintegration) as well as challenges to the role of rationality in helping us achieve a better understanding of the meaning of the human experience. All will have an impact on the role and meaning of universities. It is not a question of whether universities will change but a question of how, when, by what agency, and at what price.

Change is not new to universities. Focusing only on recent developments, it is a commonplace of our shared experience that as compared to even a half-century ago, many more of our fellow citizens participate as students in our universities. More generally, as universities grew in the past half-century not only did the internal ideals and civic functions of these institutions evolve but the links between universities and society became more varied and complex, and the influence of the state became much more marked, as it responded to its increasing investments in and the growing importance of universities.

Although acknowledged, these and other changes are often not deeply felt because university communities think of themselves as embodying a very long, very rich tradition. Nevertheless, changes have been constant. Indeed, the capacity of universities to reimagine and reinvent themselves has enabled them to persist.

As we consider questions of the role of universities in a rapidly changing environment (raising, incidentally, the question of whether universities can change quickly enough to survive as one of society's central, defining institutions), solid answers remain elusive. Universities, their curricula, and their scholarly programs should be designed to serve civic purposes, and these purposes give universities their social legitimacy. Universities cannot be defended on the grounds that they preserve a portfolio of medieval privileges or preserve the right of teachers, scholars, and students to entitlements not enjoyed by other citizens. The special freedoms and privileges enjoyed by university communities are mechanisms that enable them to meet their social responsibilities.

Only within this context is the notion of university autonomy properly understood. This autonomy is not an ancient right that must be protected at any cost. It must serve and promote the underlying civic responsibilities of universities. Thus, universities are inevitably forced to debate the relationship of their programs and commitments to the changing needs of society. We cannot and should not avoid such discussions. In particular, we must not view such discussions as undermining us or university traditions, for such dialogue reinforces our most important values. Articulating the relationship between academic freedom and the inclusive university contributes to this vital, ongoing debate.

Not everyone perceives the current role of universities in the same way, which is as it should be. Even with respect to so-called research universities, there continues to be a wide variety of competing views regarding our appropriate civic function. In some circles, for example, despite strong ties to the world outside universities and to the idea of the importance of their role in professional education, some cling to the notion of a free, isolated academic community organized around complementary ideas of a classical liberal arts curriculum and the disinterested search for new knowledge and understanding. At the same time, others consider the changing profile of universities as reflecting, in an appropriate and instrumental way, the need to provide the skills required by rapidly changing economic, social, and cultural environments. These individuals celebrate the fact that universities have left off providing a rather narrow range of scholarship and professional training to an established social elite, instead creating a more broadly based elite that can sustain economic leadership and cultural order in a new world order. If it ever was useful to talk about *the* idea of the university in the singular, it clearly makes no sense now. It is not so much *e pluribus unum* as the other way around.

More widespread than these two notions of the university is the view of nonacademics. For many citizens, universities are primarily vocational schools. In the view of parents and students, universities are a social mobility ladder where the acquisition of cultural capital has cash value in the job market. When societies view social mobility as a right of fully expressed citizenship, demand will grow for university access, whether as students, faculty, or staff – not only from individuals but also from traditionally excluded groups (for example, women, racial minorities, the disabled, and Aboriginal populations). Among the most positive features of Canadian society are its cultural diversity and its broad commitment to fair treatment and fair opportunity for all to share in both the governance and the benefits of our society. It is essential to our common sense of humanity, to the effective functioning of democratic institutions, and to cultural and economic life that we achieve as full a degree of participation as possible. Universities must make every effort to eliminate social, cultural, and economic impediments to this goal. The achievement of social justice in such an increasingly diverse polity depends on our capacity to extend not mere tolerance but also empathy and mutual respect across lines of colour, gender, religion, and ethnic background. We must strive to create a pervasive sense of inclusion and a rising sense of hope and possibility for all, because our prospects are interwoven, and we must depend on one another.

There is no denying that universities are much more inclusive than they once were. Indeed, the most obvious consequence of the transition from a small to a mass university system is the increasing heterogeneity of the university community. This heterogeneity is not, as is often implied, limited to the intellectual capacity of the students, because that would suggest that our previous criteria for student selection were purely meritocratic, which was not the case. Opportunity for participation in university life is now open to groups and individuals whose intellectual capacity was always adequate but whose socioeconomic status did not encourage or allow the option of a university education. Consequently, the notion of universities as communities of shared values has become increasingly strained – an analogy to the strains and tensions in liberal democracies where the electorate has become increasingly pluralistic. All coherent communities require some shared values, but more and more pluralistic or democratic (that is, noncoercive) societies find that the shared values in their world become fewer. Likewise in universities, certain shared values have been sustained, but others have given way in the service of meeting the needs and shaping the benefits of an ever more heterogeneous community.

Do any of these developments explain the current paradox facing universities: high public expectations and low public confidence and support? Recent popular complaints against universities include neglect of undergraduate teaching, fragmented fields of study, trivialized scholarship, conflicts of interest, imposition of political correctness, and falsification of experimental results, to say nothing of a continuing public stereotype of universities as self-indulgent, arrogant, and resistant to change. Even relative insiders seem upset. Page Smith contends that "the vast majority of the so-called research turned out in the modern university is essentially worthless," and Thomas Sowell asserts that "educators ... have proclaimed their dedication to freedom of ideas ... while turning educational institutions into bastions of dogma."[1]

I do not believe that our increasing inclusiveness, however incomplete, clumsily handled, and complex, is the problem. Criticisms are inevitable in an open society where universities have become a part of the establishment. Why not address such criticisms as attempts, in Adlai Stevenson's words, "to test whether what is, might not be better"?

If we are to directly address the matter of inclusiveness, we might do so along with what Frank Rhodes describes as the two other deep changes in universities that have resulted from their greater social engagement: professionalization and the ascendancy of science. Universities have become not only more inclusive with regard to students and faculty but also more inclusive in their curricula. They have responded to public needs by offering new fields of study: environmental policy, regional planning, gerontology, real estate management. As well, university studies have become far more professional in the scope of their curricula and far more practical in their orientation. It is not, of course, the presence of professional and practical studies that is new, but rather their dominance. Most recent additions are professional, while long-established schools of agriculture, architecture, dentistry, engineering, law, management, medicine, public communication, public health, and so on, loom larger than before in enrolment and influence. In many universities, premedical education has distorted the general pattern of undergraduate education. Even the humanities and social sciences are often splintered and divided into subspecialties in an attempt to link them more directly to specific career training.

The ascendancy of science has also changed the culture of universities. The model of scientific knowledge – abstract, quantifiable, impersonal, "value neutral" – has been adopted uncritically by other fields, and the style of teaching – factual, sequential, undebatable, and unengaging – has had an unfortunate effect not only within science but also far beyond.

On the whole, the recent benefits to society have been immense, and the changes wrought by increased inclusiveness, professionalism, and the ascendancy of science have also been great. But, along the way, some important things have been lost. As we have assumed new responsibilities and new priorities and established new partnerships with business and government, the moral influence of our universities has diminished. We should not be surprised to learn from Alexander Astin's annual surveys of first-year students' attitudes that far more of those students now believe it is more important to go to university to prepare for a well-paying career than to find a meaningful philosophy of life. But inclusiveness, professionalism, and science without a moral foundation lead to empty success. Like nations, universities need moral moorings. More people knowing more facts about more fields has nothing to do with how wisely or happily they live.

To deal with this challenge, we must reaffirm that scholarship is a public trust, and as creators of knowledge, we must also engage in explanation and application where appropriate. Most of us regard our scholarship as complete when it is published, exhibited, or performed. But we need to move beyond publication to explanation. We must become advocates for research. We must ensure that the fruits of our research are developed for the public good. And of course, we must build bridges that effectively link research to the undergraduate experience.

Finally, we must reaffirm the value of teaching as a moral vocation, because it has an impact not only on the mind but also on the character and the will. Teaching must be seen and felt to be a "calling" and not just a means of earning a living to allow us to do research. Accordingly, both the content and the method of teaching should attract our concern a great deal more than they usually do. To even begin realizing the affirmations of public trust, social service, and teaching as a moral vocation within the context of greater inclusiveness will be no easy task. Two kinds of change are necessary. First, we need to introduce programs that recognize the epistemological and ontological understanding of groups newly represented in the university community. Second, in many universities, the curriculum has escaped the faculty as a whole; it is being constructed simply by putting together the teaching specialties and preferences of individuals and departments. As a result, in more cases than we would like to admit, the curriculum fails to bring coherence to the undergraduate program, which is experienced by students as merely "one course after another." In my view, there is not much evidence that we have managed to bring the same creative energy to teaching as we have to research.

How do these challenges relate to academic freedom? At first glance, the answer is not obvious, for academic freedom has characterized university institutions that were anything but inclusive. Academic freedom simply provides university communities with the protection that must accompany teaching, independent research, and the obligation of university faculty to act as social critics. Academics should express ideas at odds with other views in the university and sometimes with the views of society and government. Academic freedom ensures that such ideas can be expressed without fear of interference or repression from outside (for example, government officials and politicians) or inside (for example, university administrators, peer review panels, and colleagues). Inclusiveness does, however, increase the tension because university communities now comprise colleagues, both faculty and students, whose priorities and shared values are more disparate. Increased levels of conflict and misunderstanding are inevitable, straining the capacity of the institution to develop common commitment and community, and creating in the wider public a vision of the institution so hopelessly mired in its own internal strife as to make it not only incapable of but also uninterested in fulfilling its civic functions.

The challenge is twofold. First, we must recognize the often positive, even healing, value of conflict, stinging social criticism, and the clash of competing visions. We should not, therefore, shut down debate on any subject of legitimate scholarship and research, even when the matter is (for example, in race-related studies) potential social dynamite. Unfortunately, too many in academia and the mass media attempt, from the radical right or the radical left, to suppress debate. It is no accident that the label "political correctness" is so popular across the entire spectrum of academic political life.

Second, the challenge to inclusiveness and academic freedom will be to decide how institutions, building on a thinner base of common social values and cultural experiences, can find mechanisms to recognize the many distinct cultural identities that form our society's increasingly complex mosaic and to sustain a secure learning environment for everyone. What moral perspectives do we need to share to reason and work together effectively? How do we define and sustain shared moral sensibilities?

This matter is not peripheral. Involved are a variety of considerations, including the fundamental liberal assumption about the autonomy and importance of the individual and of finding new and better ways to respect differences and reject domination. We perhaps should be amazed that the idea of a university has survived at all. We must recall how historically atypical it is to have sustained over time a society with many institutions that oppose and/or provide a balance to the power of the state. The idea that the state could support institutions that prevent that state's monopoly over power and truth is novel. It should not be taken for granted. It is true that we are currently experiencing some attenuation in the power of the state, but this attenuation heightens rather than reduces the need for a minimal common value centre for any community, including the university community. This connection implies institutional arrangements that are associated with liberal democracies as well as with the liberal arts. I make no apology for this connection, for I accept that liberal politics and liberal education must be tempered by two critical understandings: the human condition places some limit on the common agreements that can be reached by a group of citizens with different ideas about what is most worthy; liberal thought faces an inevitable and never entirely resolvable tension between a commitment to tolerance and to the liberty to pursue one's individual identity, and the necessary restraints to ensure the survival of the community.

These tensions are existential and will be with us as long as we remain thinking, inquiring people. I remain unflinchingly on the side of Isaiah Berlin, who maintained the thesis that liberalism has a universal claim on reason by virtue of the nature of humanity as a choice-making creature, and the thesis that liberalism is a moral and political commitment with no universal claim on reason. This contradiction denies us, as John Gray has repeatedly pointed out, the metaphysical comfort of a universal authority for a particular way of life as rational or natural or historical.[2] We are, therefore, at one with Job in rejecting the pretence of peace when our lives abound in deep conflicts and hard choices.

On another level, the real problem may be loss of faith that the academy can develop a new, even if not permanent, conception of truth transcending radical deconstructionism, the unmasking of knowledge, with a world view focused on the integration of our new and our previous understandings.

In this goal lies the great thrill of academic life. For us, truth is simply the horizon beyond which we cannot see – yet.

**Notes**
1  Thomas Sowell, *A Conflict of Visions* (New York: William Morrow and Co., 1987).
2  John Gray, *Isaiah Berlin* (Princeton, NJ: Princeton University Press, 1996).

# 5
# Academic Freedom in Social Context
*Jennie Hornosty*

In the 1960s and 1970s, great numbers of women and people from other traditionally marginalized groups entered the academy. Their presence problematized deeply held assumptions about science, knowledge, objectivity, and truth. Critiques of the prevailing scholarship revealed how women and their contributions were excluded from teaching and research. As well, judgments of academic merit were shown to be subjective, accorded only to those whose work conformed to established notions of scholarship.[1] A new discourse emerged to challenge the traditional ideas and structures that governed university life (including curriculum, power relationships, and institutional culture), which were products of a particular hegemonic masculinity. Women and others (for example, Aboriginals, blacks, other visible minorities, and lesbians and gays) began to make clear that their perspectives, values, and knowledge were excluded from the academic domain and that a radical reconceptualization of traditional academic values was necessary to encompass diversity.

Their points of view were not met with universal approval. Critics of new programs such as women's studies, black studies, and Native studies warned of the "decline" and "demise" of the liberal university. It was said that universities "engaged in drastic compromises in admissions requirements" (D'Souza 1990: 231) and that students graduated without knowledge of, or respect for, the culture of Western civilization. "The University now offers no distinctive visage to the young person ... of what an educated human being is" (Bloom 1987: 337).

This lament for traditional values of rational inquiry and the pursuit of scholarly truth continues today in many quarters. Recommendations for curriculum reviews to encompass diversity are labelled Orwellian and an interference with academic freedom. Policies of employment equity and guidelines against sexual and racial harassment are characterized as violating freedom of speech and academic freedom, and as undermining the merit principle in hiring. In the opinion of those belonging to the recently founded

Society for Academic Freedom and Scholarship (SAFS), these developments "have run rough-shod over principles of scholarly integrity and impartiality, freedom of expression and open debate, and basic fairness and democratic representation" (Brown, cited in Hodgkinson 1993: 27).

The reality is that no scientific evidence has been produced to substantiate such claims, nor has there been serious debate over these issues. Rather, the opponents have lumped together all new policies and curriculum changes under the label "political correctness," and they warn of impending dangers. According to SAFS member Hodgkinson, political correctness, which he defines as "a system of restraint, inhibition, and censorship ... deemed offensive to a radical utopian egalitarian collectivist orthodoxy grounded in a metaphysics of resentment" (1993: 24), threatens liberty and individuality. Under this rubric of political correctness, he includes employment equity policies and feminist scholarship. In his view, "Tomorrow the penalties may be more severe. Full censorship by the righteous. Utopian, collectivist, socially-engineered language and mind control. Intellectual serfdom. The Gulag and the bullet" (1993: 32).

Such inflammatory rhetoric does not lead to reasoned debate. However, this is not the first time that such sentiments have been expressed. Similar views were heard during the student protests of the 1960s and early 1970s. Opponents of radical students feared that the intellectual integrity of the university was being destroyed. They felt an urgent need to rally "to the defence of academic integrity and freedom against the enemies *within* as well as outside the academy" (Hook 1974: xviii). Then, as now, the stated goal was to reclaim the university of the past[2] – the university that valued dispassionate inquiry, preserved the canons of Western civilization, and comprised a community of scholars in pursuit of a common objective (Hoffman 1974). It was argued that the university should be a citadel of higher learning; a gender-blind and colour-blind establishment that maintained a stance of neutrality with respect to so-called nonscholarly and noneducational issues.

It is significant that pressures for change from within the academy are characterized by opponents as violating principles of academic freedom. To understand why, for example, the executive director of the Vancouver-based Fraser Institute characterized attempts to make the university more inclusive – more egalitarian – as "a loss of academic freedom and a threat to the quality of scholarship" (Walker 1993: 4), we need to deconstruct the concept of academic freedom. How is it that this *ideal*, the foundation of the modern university, can be used to silence the new scholarship, values, ideas, and practices of persons seeking change?

Principles of academic freedom in the United States first emerged to protect the university and its professoriate from outside interference (Poch 1993). The 1940 "Statement of Principles on Academic Freedom and Tenure" (AAUP

1990) sets out principles to guarantee intellectual freedom in research, teaching, publication, and extramural communication. Subsequent policies incorporated these basic values. For example, the "Policy Statement on Academic Freedom" (CAUT 1977) states that principles of academic freedom confer on academic staff the freedom to teach and to discuss, freedom to carry out research and publish the results, freedom to exercise their legal rights as citizens without jeopardizing their academic status, freedom to criticize the university and faculty association, and freedom from institutional censorship. The intent is to allow individuals to pursue scholarly endeavours without fear of reprisal.

Academic freedom does not, however, exist apart from social relations. It is not an unmediated concept; it is practised in a cultural and institutional context that includes power differences and inequalities. Principles of academic freedom have never been absolute: the history of the McCarthy witch hunts in the United States, the denial of tenure to prominent Marxist scholars, the experience of countless feminists whose scholarship was judged inadequate, the purges at McGill University and Simon Fraser University against "radical Marxists" in the sociology and political science departments – all testify that principles of academic freedom have not been applied uniformly.[3]

Clearly, principles of academic freedom take on meaning within a given socioeconomic and political context. The values, beliefs, and norms of society at large and of the governors of a university shape how these principles are interpreted and who they will protect. In looking at the response of American universities to McCarthyism, for example, Ellen Schrecker (1986: 14) writes: "The concept of academic freedom became a useful way to describe in ostensibly professional terms the permissible limits of political dissent. It created an intellectually defensible zone of political autonomy ... which ... was sufficiently circumscribed so as to exclude as unscholarly whatever political behaviour the leading members of the academic community feared might trigger outside intervention ... During periods of crisis, ... professors and administrators responded by revising the normally vague definition of academic freedom to exclude in a surprisingly explicit way the types of behaviour the rest of the community did not like." In other words, what is not made explicit in discussions about academic freedom is that definitions of scholarship and knowledge are in large part value-based and depend on assumptions about truth, human nature, science, objectivity, and so on held by those who define the canons of the day. Moreover, these unstated assumptions are seldom subject to scrutiny or critical analysis. Yet, despite the shady history of its practice, academic freedom is considered integral to the mission of a university. Academics still fervently believe that academic freedom is worth protecting (Tight 1988).

If the principles of academic freedom are not absolute but subject to interpretation, then we need to examine the epistemological assumptions underlying different interpretations of academic freedom. It is my contention that our notion of academic freedom (as well as human rights and civil liberties) is based on fundamental precepts of classical liberal theory.[4] That is, liberal precepts of equality, individualism, and freedom have shaped our understanding and expectations of academic freedom. In short, equality means treating everyone the same, individual rights are antithetical to group rights, and individual freedom and autonomy supersede all other goals.

Liberal theory is based on a conception of human beings as rational creatures who ontologically exist before society. That is, their essential characteristics, needs, desires, and capacities are natural properties, unaffected by social circumstances; human nature is therefore immutable. The atomistic individual strives alone for freedom, self-realization, and achievement of self-interest, and freedom means the absence of external constraints. In other words, in the liberal tradition, the individual has moral priority over the community. From this perspective, individuality contrasts with sociality: there is no comprehension of a socialist individual whose individualism develops within a community (Wood 1972: 128-9).

If one accepts the basic liberal values of autonomy, equality, individual dignity, rationality, and self-actualization, certain kinds of social organization follow. For example, equality means equality of opportunity, a formal equality entitling individuals to compete for scarce resources. Both failure and success are the result of individual effort. Rationality is a property of abstract individuals and thus is not defined by group norms or social structures. Because resources are limited and individuals seek to maximize their self-interest, the good society is one that "must protect the dignity of each individual and promote individual autonomy and self-fulfilment ... The good society should allow each individual the maximum freedom from interference by others (Jaggar 1983: 33). From the liberal perspective, freedom means the "active proprietorship of one's person and capacities" and requires "a guaranteed freedom from arbitrary arrest, trial, and imprisonment, and the right to due process of law ... Property in one's mental and spiritual person require[s] freedom of speech, publication" (Macpherson 1970: 142).

Liberalism does not accord significance to difference in individual circumstances – to the rank, class, race, or sex of individuals (Jaggar 1983: 32). Civil liberties are extended to all; however, there is no recognition of the basic structural inequality inherent in a class and gendered society. Differences of power and structural inequalities that circumscribe people's lives are ignored in the liberal discussion of equality. The individualism in liberal thought is, as C.B. Macpherson demonstrated, a possessive individualism: "The individual was seen neither as a moral whole, nor as part of a larger social whole, but as an owner of himself" (1970: 3). In other words, liberal thought offers little as a foundation on which to build principles of obligation and social responsibility.

If the dominant interpretation of academic freedom is rooted in liberal principles, it is clear why initiatives for curriculum change and policies essential for an inclusive university are opposed as violations of individual rights and freedoms: the individual referred to in such discourse is the atomistic individual conceptualized in liberal thought; systemic inequalities inherent in the traditional university culture are simply not acknowledged.

A basic question, then, is whether notions of individuality and freedom can exist apart from liberal discourse. Can principles of diversity and inclusiveness coexist with academic freedom? Karl Marx provides a useful framework for such considerations (1964; 1970). Unlike the atomistic individual in liberal theory, the individual for Marx is first a species-being: that is, a social being who consciously transforms the world. Individuals are not products of some pre-existing essence; rather, individuals assume their identities in and through society.

According to Marx, the individual is both shaped by and shapes cultural norms, values, and practices; self-realization is thus achieved through community. This species-being can only be understood in terms of the whole of social relations: it is through praxis at a given historical moment that the individual appropriates external reality as human reality. As Wood (1972) points out, in Marxist thought, there is no antithesis between the individual and society. Realizing one's human potential is possible only in relationships with others. A social being contrasts sharply with the self-sufficient, egoistic individual of liberal thought.

For Marx, freedom is more than the absence of external constraints. "In the relation 'individual-society,' freedom means ... a conscious shaping by men [sic] of the social conditions of their existence and so eliminating the impersonal power of alienated, reified social forces" (Walicki 1983: 53). In liberalism, equality of opportunity becomes the sole basis on which to enshrine individual rights, because in liberal thought "freedom is considered to be unaffected by the unequal constraints ... that are necessarily imposed on men [sic] by the realities of their social and economic status, by property and class differentials" (Wood 1972: 114). Within a Marxist framework, a precondition for individual freedom is equality of condition, which requires much more than the elimination of legal barriers: it requires the creation of a level playing field that eliminates structural barriers to opportunity.

The ideology of equal opportunity opened universities to members of nontraditional groups, but it did not change the organizational culture or affect the traditional power structure of the institution. Thus, the current struggle for an inclusive university challenges traditional cultures and structures. The controversy over the legitimacy of a diversified curriculum and employment equity policies, while couched in terms of academic freedom, is in truth a struggle over different conceptions of the university.

At the same time, underlying the debate over academic freedom and the inclusive university are views of justice, freedom, and equality rooted in different philosophical traditions and different views of society and the social order. One way to explain this difference is to look at differing notions of the individual and freedom. Those who argue that reforming policies and curriculum violates academic freedom adhere to a liberal notion of individual rights and freedoms. Those who advocate such changes adhere to something like the Marxist notion of social individuality.[5] At the same time, it is important to recognize that these conceptions operate tacitly; most people are unaware that their interpretations are shaped by presuppositions that rarely receive critical examination (Hawkesworth 1990).

Academic freedom is an important ideal, but what does it really mean when universities have been dominated by white male elites who define knowledge, curriculum, ways of being, and the organizational culture in their image (Smith 1987)? What does it mean to talk of academic freedom in a class society with multiple layers of inequality (Fisk 1972)?

Although framed in terms of academic freedom, the actual debate is over the nature of the university: its organizational culture, the range of its scholarship, the composition of its student body and faculty. Criticism within the academy, as well as federal and provincial government initiatives, led to the implementation of new policies. Among the most controversial of these initiatives are employment equity and discrimination and harassment policies, where opponents argue that such policies violate academic freedom and are thus inappropriate on university campuses.

Traditional liberal assumptions are at the core of this argument. The civil libertarian approach to individual rights assumes that all people are decontextualized, rights-bearing individuals; structural differences in power and equality between social groups are not considered problematic. Equality in liberal theory refers to a legal equality where all individuals have the legal right to compete for scarce resources. This equality of opportunity means that individuals alone are responsible for their success and failure. Theoretically, all have a right to higher education and an academic career. If some feel marginalized or are made uncomfortable by the existing environment, then their failure to adjust is the source of their problem. Similarly, if someone is not hired for a position, it is the fault of the applicant, and never the result of a bias in the system.

Civil libertarians assume that competition – between people or ideas – takes place on a level playing field. They believe in a free marketplace where ideas and people are subject to rational, objective evaluation. Thus, the truth and the best always triumph. Policies that dispute this approach interfere with individual rights. As well, civil libertarians argue for the free expression of ideas, contending that harmful, false, politically unacceptable, or dangerous ideas can be refuted by counterarguments (Schrank 1994: 9). On the surface, this position is appealing until we realize that not all voices have equal opportunities to be heard. The dominant ideology of a society inevitably determines the topics worthy of debate.

It is also said that members of traditionally marginalized groups are free to compete against white males for positions: the most qualified person will get the job. There again is a presupposition of a "universal culture" where true equality of opportunity exists. But as others have explained, equality of condition is not an attribute of capitalist society (Macpherson 1970; Wood 1972; Jaggar 1983), where the division of labour and structures of inequality limit one's options and choices. In such a society, complete individual freedom is an illusion; partial freedom is available only to the extent that those with power and resources do not limit the actions of others who possess less power and fewer resources. Only those with power bestowed by class, race, and gender are able to privilege their rights.

Similarly, the dominant culture within the academy defines knowledge and thus decides the ideas worthy of discussion. Free expression of ideas is available only to those whose ideas fall within the parameters of the approved discourse; unorthodox critiques are ignored or dismissed as nonscholarly. Accordingly, academic freedom fails to protect those whose ideas and scholarship are deemed subjective, irrational, incompetent, and without merit (Dixon 1976; Schrecker 1986).

By and large these liberal beliefs are shared by most of the academic community, and they justify the claim that equity policies not only are unnecessary but also interfere with academic freedom. In truth, treating people equitably requires taking into account structural differences to eliminate the inequities of the past. To ensure equity, which is a prerequisite for the inclusive university, we need to recognize that the university structure and its organizational culture have traditionally privileged some and marginalized others; we need to go beyond theoretical concepts of equality by eliminating systemic barriers that hinder the equal participation of members of all groups; we need to create an equality of condition, not merely an equality of opportunity. Of course, such an approach is anathema to those who view the world through a liberal lens. Given their assumptions about the world, anything that changes the traditional structure interferes with individual rights and academic freedom.

Liberal assumptions about individuality, freedom, and equality are the hallmarks of the liberal university. As well, a theory of knowledge based on tenets of positivism dominates academic scholarship. Research is premised on a belief in universal truth and a methodology of hypothesis testing. Through this scientific model, the expert discovers the facts. This model runs counter to more contemporary theories of knowledge that place importance on the knowing subject. From this perspective, there can be many truths. Within this framework, knowledge is socially constructed; facts do not exist independently of interpretations rooted in theoretical perspectives and assumptions about human nature. Those academics who accept a theory of knowledge that recognizes how different standpoints can shape varying interpretations of truth and reality are more likely to be proponents of the inclusive university.[6]

Although such a university does not yet exist, one can identify its essential features:[7] the curriculum would recognize the diversity of people's experience; the pedagogy would be critical and progressive; teaching would empower students; the organizational culture would be based on human rights principles that prohibit unwarranted discrimination; and debate about new directions in research and scholarship would be ongoing.[8]

Creating an inclusive university would require deconstructing the traditional power structure to reveal how it reinforces white male privilege (Aisenberg and Harrington 1988; Smith 1987) and capitalist social relations (Dixon 1976; Fisk 1972). An inclusive university would legitimize different voices and accept a variety of methodologies and ways of knowing. It would recognize as valuable and incorporate into existing scholarship ideas that reflect experiences of diversity. This revisioning would require critical rethinking of how corporate interests have influenced academic work. A central question would be "Knowledge for whom and knowledge of what?" As Bannerji (1991) argues, when we transmit knowledge, we do not merely supply information or teach "facts," we also create new ways of seeing and interpretations rooted in particular ideologies.

An inclusive university would provide a culture where people from diverse backgrounds and experiences feel they belong, which means we would need policy and curriculum changes. Such changes might well entail limits on some types of behaviour or attitudes. Debate about ideas should flourish, but deliberately humiliating or hurting others because of their views cannot be acceptable. This restriction is not, contrary to what some may claim, a violation of academic freedom. As John Cowan succinctly says, "There is no academic freedom to harass. There is no academic freedom to be disruptive ... There is no academic freedom to intimidate, there is no academic freedom to interfere with the academic freedom of others" (1994: 7). The culture of the inclusive university would be based on values of equity; that is, an equality of condition and the elimination of all systemic barriers.

Notions of equity, diversity, and inclusiveness begin with a set of premises about individualism, freedom, and rights that take as given the existence of deeply rooted inequalities in social structure. As Pottinger (1977:

42) shows, "systemic forms of exclusion, inattention, and discrimination cannot be remedied in any meaningful way, in any reasonable length of time, simply by ensuring a future benign neutrality with regard to race and sex. This would perpetuate indefinitely the grossest inequities of past discrimination." It is to redress these structural inequalities that employment equity policies have come about.

These developments do not mean, however, that the inclusive university compromises academic freedom or the merit principle. Similarly, policies against harassment and violence do not interfere with the mission of the university as a place for dialogue and the exchange of ideas. Rather, such policies change the parameters of acceptable behaviour to eliminate sexism, racism, homophobia, and intimidation. One may argue that such policies violate an individual's freedom of speech, but they do not infringe on one's right to teach, research, or publish in the area of one's expertise. Moreover, we need to remember that free speech is one value among others and needs to be balanced against other values such as respect for others, tolerance, and a more egalitarian vision of justice (Hutchinson 1994).

Many have argued that academic freedom is necessary to ensure the right to critical thought and to challenge traditional orthodoxies: feminist theory and women's studies programs have generally benefited from principles of academic freedom (McCormack 1987). Yet as long as liberal precepts inform our notions of the individual and freedom, cries of "a violation of academic freedom" will rise against attempts to transform the traditional liberal university into a more inclusive one. The idea that academic freedom is the right to pursue knowledge and truth as one sees it should be preserved. Principles of academic freedom are necessary for an inclusive university, but they are not sufficient. We need to change the social and institutional climate of the university so that academic freedom incorporates an understanding of the social individual – the individual as shaped by social context.

These issues are some of the major difficulties in discussions of academic freedom and the inclusive university. They centre on different conceptions of equality, freedom, justice, rights, and the individual. The hegemony of liberal thought makes it difficult to deconstruct academic freedom and conceptualize other ways of understanding the relationship of the individual in a community. Because our understanding of academic freedom has been decontextualized, we often fail to see how the values, beliefs, and norms that govern the university at a given time shape the practice of academic freedom.

Seen through a liberal lens, academic freedom will invariably conflict with attempts to make the university more inclusive. However, when we acknowledge that principles of academic freedom do not exist apart from social relations but rather are mediated by specific cultural and institutional arrangements, we discover that academic freedom need not be at odds with the values of the inclusive university. Academic freedom in social context means recognizing that differences in power and inequality can obstruct the pursuit of equal opportunity and that the elimination of systemic barriers may require some individual rights to give way to group rights.

Academic freedom should never include the right to "make others uncomfortable, to injure, by expression, anyone's self-esteem, and to create, by expression, atmospheres in which some may not feel welcome or accepted" as suggested by those professors who signed the "Trent University Statement on Free Inquiry and Expression."[9] In a context of unequal power, sarcasm, jokes, anger, insults, and put-downs can subordinate and silence others (Ramazanoglu 1987: 65).

The notion of a social individual and principles of equity are basic to the inclusive university. Inclusiveness implies the right to participate in a discourse that is one's own and to work and study in an environment where one is subject, not object; where one is not produced as the other, as "different," but where one is acknowledged as human (Bannerji 1991). To bring about this change, we must critically examine the liberal precepts on which we build our notions of academic freedom, equality, and higher education.

**Notes**

1 Some feminist academics had difficulty getting tenure and promotion. Their work used new methodologies that transcended narrowly defined disciplinary boundaries and, according to those who judged their work unworthy, took trivial matters as subjects. Similarly, the work of Marxist scholars was considered nonacademic and biased.
2 Although many articles describe the traditional or liberal university as the height of the "golden age" of higher education, that age was noteworthy not for its democracy but for its elitism. Teachers taught an established canon and students were required to learn it.
3 CAUT argued that academic freedom was violated at both McGill University and Simon Fraser University. Asserting that academic freedom principles exist did nothing to change the views of the majority of the professoriate, especially at McGill (see Dixon 1976).
4 Classical liberal theory includes the political theories of seventeenth- and eighteenth-century thinkers such as Thomas Hobbes, John Locke, and J.S. Mill, who provided the foundation of liberalism.
5 Here, I follow Hawkesworth's argument (1990).
6 German sociologist Max Weber (1949) offers the useful construct of the ideal-type. He developed this construct as a way of understanding the relationship between the idea of something and its approximation or divergence in reality. The ideal-type is thus a mental construct and "in itself is like a *utopia* which has been arrived at by the analytical accentuation of certain elements of reality" (1949: 90). We can develop the idea of an inclusive university by arranging the characteristics or traits of inclusivity into an ideal-type construct.
7 One of the difficulties in discussing the inclusive university is that it has not been concretely defined. The notion is used in juxtaposition to the traditional university, where faculty taught the Western canons (a specific body of knowledge that all students must master) and privileged scientific inquiry so that the researcher was considered an objective observer engaged in the pursuit of a "scientific truth." The traditional university was built around the notion of education for an elite: it was intended to be an ivory tower, unconcerned with the needs of the wider society.

8   I have indicated in general terms five of the most obvious features. There are undoubtedly others.
9   This document was publicly circulated at Trent University in response to the Ontario government's "Framework regarding Prevention of Harassment and Discrimination in Ontario Universities."

## References

Aisenberg, N., and M. Harrington. 1988. *Women of Academe: Outsiders in the Sacred Grove.* Amherst: University of Massachusetts Press.
American Association of University Professors (AAUP). July/August 1990. "Academic Freedom and Artistic Expression." *Academe* 76: 13.
Bannerji, H. 1991. "But Who Speaks for Us? Experience and Agency in Conventional Feminist Paradigms." In *Unsettling Relations: The University as a Site for Feminist Struggles,* ed. H. Bannerji et al., 67-107. Boston: South End Press.
Bloom, A. 1987. *The Closing of the American Mind.* New York: Simon and Schuster.
Canadian Association of University Professors (CAUT). 1997. "Policy Statement on Academic Freedom." Ottawa, ON.
Cowan, J.S. 1994. "Lessons from the Fabrikant File: A Report to the Board of Governors of Concordia University." Montreal, QC.
Dixon, M. 1976. *Things Which Are Done in Secret.* Montreal: Black Rose Books.
D'Souza, D. 1990. *Illiberal Education: The Politics of Race and Sex on Campus.* New York: Free Press.
Fisk, M. 1972. "Academic Freedom in Class Society." In *The Concept of Academic Freedom,* ed. E. Pincoffs, 5-26. Austin, TX: University of Texas Press.
Hawkesworth, M.E. 1988. "The Politics of Knowledge: Sexual Harassment and Academic Freedom Reconsidered." In *Academic Freedom and Responsibility,* ed. M. Tight, 17-30. Stony Stratford, England: Open University Press.
Hawkesworth, M.E. 1990. "The Affirmative Action Debate and Conflicting Conceptions of Individuality." In *Hypathia Reborn,* ed. A. Alhibri and M. Simons, 135-55. Bloomington: Indiana University Press.
Hodgkinson, C. 1993. "Taking Political Correctness Seriously." In *In Defence of Academic Freedom and Scholarship. Fraser Forum. (Critical Issues Bulletin III),* ed. M. Walker, 24-32. Vancouver: Fraser Institute.
Hoffman, R. 1974. "The Irrelevance of Relevance." In *The Idea of a Modern University,* ed. S. Hook, P. Kurtz, and M. Todorovich, 107-18. Buffalo: Prometheus Books.
Hook, S. 1974. Introduction to *The Idea of a Modern University.* In *The Idea of a Modern University,* ed. S. Hook, P. Kurtz, and M. Todorovich, xvii-xix. Buffalo: Prometheus Books.
Hutchinson, A. 1994. "Like Lunches, Speech Is Never Free." *University Affairs.* June/July: 12
Jaggar, A. 1983. *Feminist Politics and Human Nature.* Totowa, NJ: Rowman and Allanheld.
Macpherson, C.B. 1970. *The Political Theory of Possessive Individualism.* London: Oxford University Press.
Marx, Karl. 1964. *The Economic & Philosophic Manuscripts of 1844.* Ed. Dirk Struik. New York: International Publishers.
–. 1970. *The German Ideology.* Ed. C.J. Arthur. New York: International Publishers.
McCormack, T. 1987. "Feminism, Women's Studies and the New Academic Freedom." In *Women and Education (A Canadian Perspective),* ed. J. Gaskell and A. McLaren, 289-303. Calgary: Detselig Enterprises.
Poch, R. 1993. *Academic Freedom in American Higher Education (Rights, Responsibilities and Limitations).* ASHE-ERIC Higher Education Report, No. 4. Washington, DC.
Pottinger, J.S. 1977. "The Drive toward Equality." In *Reverse Discrimination,* ed. B. Gross, 41-53. Buffalo: Prometheus Books.
Ramazanoglu, C. 1987. "Sex and Violence in Academic Life or You Can Keep a Good Woman Down." In *Women, Violence and Social Control,* ed. J. Hanmer and M. Maynard, 61-74. London: Macmillan Press.
Schrank, B. 1994. "Academic Freedom and the Inclusive University." *CAUT Bulletin.* May: 9-11.

Schrecker, E. 1986. *No Ivory Tower (McCarthyism and the Universities)*. New York: Oxford University Press.

Smith, D. 1987. "A Peculiar Eclipsing: Women's Exclusion from Man's Culture." In *The Everyday World as Problematic*, by D. Smith, 17-43. Toronto: University of Toronto Press.

Tight, M. 1988. "So What Is Academic Freedom?" In *Academic Freedom and Responsibility*, ed. M. Tight, 114-32. Stony Stratford, England: Open University Press.

Walicki, A. 1983. "Marx and Freedom." *New York Review of Books*. 24 November: 50-5.

Walker, M., ed. 1993. *In Defence of Academic Freedom and Scholarship. Fraser Forum (Critical Issues Bulletin III)*. Vancouver: Fraser Institute.

Weber, M. 1949. *The Methodology of the Social Sciences*. Trans. and ed. E. Shils and H. Finch. Glencoe, IL: Free Press.

Wood, E.M. 1972. *Mind and Politics*. Berkeley: University of California Press.

# 6

# The Exclusive University and Academic Freedom

*Michiel Horn*

Overall, the history of the Canadian university has been a history of exclusion.[1] This is particularly true of the composition of the faculty. As recently as 1960, women, all of them white and Gentile, made up only one in seven full-time faculty, while ethnic minorities were still little in evidence. Anti-Semitism was declining, but only in the 1960s did the appointment of Jews become commonplace; non-Caucasian faculty members then could probably be counted on the fingers of one hand.

The extent to which members of such groups felt hampered in their academic freedom is a matter for speculation. In the absence of hard evidence, we may assume that they shared the freedom available to the majority within the classroom and laboratory, but that on the whole, women felt inhibited in faculty meetings and were even less eager than other academics to draw attention to themselves *hors les murs*. A major problem was getting inside the walls in the first place.

In institutions predominantly staffed and almost exclusively run by men, women were still outsiders. One indication was the habit of everyone associated with universities to use the male pronoun when discussing professors and to make it clear that in appointments one was looking for men. (It goes without saying that he was of British or, in the French-language institutions, of French ancestry.) Far into the twentieth century, the ideal academic was male. Women were subjected to discrimination before and after appointment. Often expected to remain single, they usually had lower salaries than male colleagues and served longer before gaining promotion. Many never moved beyond the lower ranks and never gained tenure. Rarely did they protest. The biologist Dixie Pelluet at Dalhousie University complained more than once against being paid below the floor for her rank, but she appears to have been unusual. Part of a minority, women had reason to be even more cautious than other academics.[2]

Thanks to Judith Fingard, we know more about faculty women at Dalhousie than at most other Canadian universities. "For women, it did matter who the president was," Fingard writes. "His views on appointments were decisive." Stanley Mackenzie (president from 1911 to 1931), who had taught at Bryn Mawr, appointed several women to the academic staff, among them the scientists Merle Colitt and Dixie Pelluet, but his successor, Carleton Stanley (1931-45), was "ambivalent" in his view of faculty women, and A.E. Kerr (1945-63) was "very hostile."[3]

Kerr's attitude emerges in an exchange with R.A. MacKay in 1946. MacKay mentioned as a possible candidate for appointment Elisabeth Wallace, then teaching political science at Toronto. "I have not ... raised the question with Miss Wallace," MacKay added, "since I thought it desirable to clear with you whether there would be any objection to taking on a woman, assuming, of course, that she were fully qualified and ... [had] the personality to handle the classes." "Your suspicion is correct that I do not wish to have too large a percentage of women on the staff," Kerr replied. "When we are choosing teachers with the date of registration within a couple of weeks, however, we are obliged to take what we can get and hope for the best."[4]

Wallace did not join Dalhousie. She was wise not to. Unfriendly as the University of Toronto may have been to faculty women, it was less so than Dalhousie under Kerr. During his presidency, three policies were introduced that directly discriminated against women. One, in 1946, reduced the age of retirement of faculty women from sixty-five to sixty. (Men were retired at sixty-five.) In 1950, prompted by Pelluet's complaints about her salary, a second policy change forced faculty women to resign if they married a faculty member, and in 1955, a third policy change, introduced after a psychologist asked for maternity leave, forced them to resign if they married, period. In each case, they could be reappointed, but only on annual contracts. (The age of retirement was raised to sixty-five in 1956, but the rule against marriage lasted until 1966, and the rule against marrying a faculty member until 1970.)

The experiences of two historians at UBC, Sylvia Thrupp and Margaret Ormsby, demonstrate the importance of the role of the president. A UBC graduate who took a doctorate at the University of London, Thrupp returned to her alma mater in 1936 as an instructor. Although it was customary for holders of a doctoral degree to have at least the rank of assistant professor, she was annually reappointed as an instructor until 1945. Having won a Guggenheim fellowship, she was on leave at the time of her promotion to assistant professor. She did not return, instead joining the faculty of the University of Chicago and in time achieving international distinction as a medievalist. Someone who knew Thrupp explained to me that her department head at UBC, Walter Sage, was willing to hire women but did not think they should be encouraged unduly. Without his recommendation, neither further promotions nor salary increases were likely to come Thrupp's way.[5]

Also a UBC graduate, Margaret Ormsby took her PhD at Bryn Mawr, eventually returning to UBC as a sessional lecturer in 1943. She was replacing F.H. Soward, who was on wartime leave with External Affairs. When he returned, classes were swollen by veterans, and she stayed on. She gained promotion to the rank of assistant professor in 1946, associate professor in 1949, and full professor in 1955. In 1964, she became department head, a position she held until her retirement ten years later.[6]

Except for its slow start, partly explained by the Depression, Ormsby's career developed typically. Yet she might, like Thrupp, have suffered as a result of Sage's attitude toward faculty women except for one thing: she caught the eye of the president, N.A.M. (Larry) MacKenzie, who served from 1944 until 1962 and fancied himself a judge of merit. "Larry used a free hand with promotions and salary increases, not always bothering with any formal channel of communication," P.B. Waite comments. "Margaret Ormsby heard of her promotion to assistant professor, not from her department head nor from the dean of Arts, but from Larry MacKenzie. Sage was surprised. Her increases and promotions all seemed to come from this same source. Larry liked to reward talent."[7] By this token, of course, if MacKenzie didn't recognize it, it wasn't talent.

Patchy information about other universities suggests that Thrupp's experience was more common than Ormsby's. Promotions, salary increases, and tenure were more readily available to men. In her memoirs, the Coleridge scholar Kathleen Coburn recalls the attitude of the principal of Victoria College, University of Toronto, Walter Brown: "He would never appoint a woman to the permanent staff of the College. In fairly short order three men, with no more experience or academic qualifications, received permanent appointments over my head." She decided to outwait Brown: he would not be there forever. After fourteen years, she got a permanent appointment.[8]

During the presidency of W.C. Murray (1908-37), the record of women at the University of Saskatchewan was better than that at many other universities. One reason may have been that his daughters sought academic careers. Both joined the staff in the 1930s, Jean in Saskatoon, Lucy in Regina, with their father initially paying their salaries out of his own pocket.[9]

In 1934, Murray appointed Hilda Neatby, her PhD in hand, as an instructor at Regina College. She taught fourteen hours a week and handled two correspondence courses, for which she earned $100 per month plus room and board. In 1936, she was promoted to the rank of assistant professor and given a tenured appointment. Her teaching load remained unchanged. Ten years later, when she moved to the main campus, she was not the first choice of the department head, George Simpson. President J.S. Thomson wrote to Simpson's dean, "Simpson still wants [Charles] Lightbody – to avoid excessive femininity in his staff." Jean Murray was already there; could the department bear the presence of two women? But there was resistance to Lightbody on other grounds, and lacking a "suitable man," Simpson relented.[10]

Neatby herself, as head of Saskatchewan's history department from 1958 to 1969, appointed only one woman during that time. Michael Hayden comments: "There were not that many [women] around to appoint and Hilda was worried about male backlash because the History Department had three women, more than any [other on] campus." She joined the CAUT's status of women committee when it was founded in 1965 and helped to write its first interim report on discrimination against female professors.[11]

While UBC and Saskatchewan had by the 1940s made permanent room for female historians, other universities excluded them until the 1960s. Margaret Banks, who enrolled in the University of Toronto's doctoral program in 1949, recalled the attitude that prevailed: "Well, that is fine, you can come and take your PhD if you want to, but, of course, you realize you won't be able to get a teaching job in the university because university history departments don't hire women." She completed her doctorate in 1953, but having been turned down by departments in "every university in Canada," she settled for work as an archivist and librarian.[12]

The University of Toronto history department made Jill Ker Conway its first permanent female member in 1964. She has written about her efforts to gain equality with her male peers. Only in 1970 did she succeed, because of intervention from senior administrators.[13] Jean Burnet, who joined Toronto in the 1940s to teach sociology, has written of that institution, "Women who aspired to academic careers were told straightforwardly that they should not set their sights too high: that, for example, many years of service and high scholarly productivity might possibly lead as far as an associate professorship. Nor should they hope for many women colleagues."[14] The faculty club was closed to them until it moved out of Hart House in the 1950s.

Well into the twentieth century, Jewish men had even more difficulty than Gentile women in gaining university appointments. In 1848, McGill appointed Abraham de Sola to a lectureship in Hebrew and Oriental languages and promoted him to the rank of professor five years later. There seems to have been no other Jew on the full-time faculty before Karl Stern, a refugee from Nazi Germany, joined McGill in 1940.[15]

In 1911, the University of Toronto had an opportunity to appoint Lewis Namier, a brilliant scholar of Polish birth, who in time became one of the twentieth century's preeminent historians of Britain. Asked by President Sir Robert Falconer for advice, J.W. Flavelle wrote that he did not like "the choice of a Polish Jew as an interpreter of history, and I presume constitutional history to our young men." He doubted that a foreigner could understand British institutions: "He may have an intellectual perception of them, yet not understand them." In view of Namier's academic record, Flavelle agreed to a year's trial appointment, but Gilbert Jackson got the job. He might have taken only second-class honours, but he was British and a Gentile.[16]

Before the Second World War, only a handful of Jews, perhaps no more than a dozen in all, gained academic appointments in Canada. Academic anti-Semitism was mostly of the more or less genteel variety, willing sometimes to accept individual Jews but worried about signs of Jewish influence. Martin Gelber, an undergraduate at the University of Toronto in the early 1930s, wrote to Frank Underhill in 1936: "The Canadian universities are full of anti-Semites who would furiously reject the application [of the term to them], but who are consistently conscience [sic] of Jewish inroads into the cultural life of our country." Marvin's brother Lionel taught on a replacement basis at the University of Toronto during the war but did not get a permanent position. When Leon Edel, who had been an undergraduate at McGill University, returned from graduate studies already working on the Henry James project that would win him international renown, he could find no university post in Canada. Bora Laskin gained appointment at the University of Toronto only after an extraordinary declaration of loyalty was required of him by his department head. The first Jew to be appointed to a permanent position in the University of Toronto history department was Morris Zaslow in 1952. Not surprisingly, young Jews who wanted academic careers often left for the United States.[17]

Ernest Sirluck has characterized as "polite" the anti-Semitism he experienced at the two universities where he studied. One was the University of Manitoba, where he was an undergraduate from 1935 to 1940; the other was the University of Toronto, which he attended as a graduate student from 1940 to 1942. Jews were somewhat suspect, but hostility was stronger toward Judaism and Judaic tradition, which were resented as challenges to the prevailing Christian outlook. Albert Rose, an undergraduate at Toronto from 1935 to 1939 who joined its faculty of social work in 1948, concurred in this assessment and its corollary: observant Jews had a harder time than those who were not conspicuously devout.[18]

In 1946, when Sirluck became a lecturer in University College, he was the first Jew to be appointed in an English department at a Canadian university. He also had offers from Queen's and the University of Western Ontario, but he was told by Fulton Anderson of the University of Toronto's philosophy department that "a Jew would not be happy at either institution."[19] Whether this claim would have been true for Queen's is hard to say: Israel Halperin had been appointed there in 1939.

Anti-Semitism helps to explain the dismal record of Canadian universities in respect of refugees from Nazism. By the outbreak of war, sixteen refugee academics had been appointed, in most cases initially with funds supplied by the Carnegie Foundation. The University of Toronto appointed six, Dalhousie University three, and the University of Saskatchewan two, one of whom, the chemist and later Nobel Prize winner Gerhard Herzberg, soon moved to the University of Toronto. Of the sixteen, five were identifiably Jewish, and one, Lothar Richter, was a "baptized non-Aryan." Six were not Jewish; the ethnic or religious background of the other four is not stated. Though married to a Jew, Herzberg was not one himself. Two of the sixteen were women. A few refugees gained university positions in the war years; the total appointed between 1933 and 1945 barely exceeded twenty.[20]

McGill University did not appoint a refugee until 1940. In July 1938, T.W.L. MacDermot, who had taught history at McGill before assuming the principalship of Upper Canada College, offered the opinion that weaknesses in the faculty of arts and science might be corrected with the aid of a few refugees.[21] This suggestion went nowhere. When Karl Stern, a convert to Roman Catholicism, gained appointment, he did so in medicine.

Principal Lewis Douglas's attitude to refugees or, more accurately, to their potential for controversy, emerges in a January 1939 memorandum. The registrar, T.H. Matthews, had asked whether McGill University's dean should adopt a policy to deal with German-Jewish students and whether the issue should be raised at the next meeting of the NCCU in the hope that Canadian universities might make "a really good Samaritan gesture across the Atlantic." Douglas replied, "This is a controversial, even dangerous subject, in which much embarrassment might develop from public discussion."[22] If the admission of German Jewish students seemed to be this problematic, it is unsurprising that McGill University, in common with most other universities, did little or nothing to help refugee faculty.

The universities were not solely responsible for this worse than niggardly policy. Budgetary woes hampered them in taking on new faculty, but more important, the federal government in the 1930s placed huge obstacles in the way of refugees and immigrants. Anti-Semitism had a part in this obstruction, but high unemployment seemed to argue against the admission of people who might do work that could be done by Canadians. In support of a restrictive policy, the historian G.F.G. Stanley stated in 1938 that it would be a mistake to admit academic refugees if this action meant that the few available teaching jobs would be taken by European Jews. A troubled economy bred deeply ungenerous attitudes.[23]

Before 1960, scholars and scientists of non-Caucasian origin were rarely if ever appointed to university positions. Information on this subject is difficult to obtain, but it seems that when the biologist Howard McCurdy joined the University of Windsor as a lecturer in 1959, he was the first Canadian of African ancestry to be appointed to a university position in Canada. The University of Toronto appointed two black sociologists, Daniel Hill and B.A. McFarlane, in the academic year 1960-1. Both were in contractually limited positions and left the university after one year, McFarlane later joining Carleton University.[24]

Members of other nonwhite groups were very slow to find their way into academe. It seems that no one of Aboriginal, East or South Asian, or Middle Eastern origin gained a university position before 1960. This situation may have resulted in part from a lack of candidates, but it appears that well into the 1960s, prejudice alone was enough to keep them out of university positions.[25]

The near-exclusion of non-Caucasians raises the same issues as the treatment of women or Jews. To discriminate against people on the ground of ethnicity or religion or sex, matters not central to the academic enterprise, is as objectionable as discriminating against them for their opinions. Because members of these groups offer a wide range of perspectives, their exclusion artificially diminishes the quality and extent of discussion and debate, weakening academic freedom.

Although the experiences of faculty women and members of other groups were not uniformly negative, the evidence indicates that into the second half of the twentieth century, discrimination was common both in hiring and in career paths. The effects are or should be beyond dispute. Provided those members of a minority group who are appointed feel isolated and vulnerable, they will probably not assert themselves. Academic freedom does not thrive in an atmosphere of insecurity.

Where members of identifiable minorities laboured under no disadvantages, their relief was less a matter of formal policy than of the practices of presidents and boards. The rule of *men* and not of law prevailed. A benevolent autocracy is preferable to one less benign, but it is still autocracy, and autocracies are not known for the freedom exercised by those who dwell in their shadow. Boards and presidents changed; who knew what the future held? All academics were aware of this uncertainty, but the most vulnerable were most disposed to heed it. Keeping a low profile, staying close to the ground, not sticking one's neck out: the metaphors capture the behaviour of minority groups even more than of academics generally.

By the early 1960s, a growing number of academics were arguing for greater faculty participation in university government. There were no women among them, and the only Jews were Bora Laskin and McGill University's Maxwell Cohen, by then very much academic elder statesmen. To challenge the citadels of power, a sense of belonging may not be essential, but it certainly helps.

**Notes**

1  I am grateful to the following people for their comments on drafts of this paper: Irving Abella, Jean Burnet, Judith Fingard, Stanley Brice Frost, Alison Prentice, and Ernest Sirluck. My wife, Cornelia Schuh, commented helpfully as well.

2  Dalhousie University Archives (DUA), Board of Governors, Minutes 1945-50, meeting of 6 December 1949; executive committee, meeting on 13 January 1950; Dixie Pelluet to A.E. Kerr, 25 November 1952, quoted in Judith Fingard, "Gender and Inequality at Dalhousie: Faculty Women before 1950," *Dalhousie Review* 64 (1984-5): 696; Jill McCalla Vickers and

June Adam, *But Can You Type?* (Toronto and Vancouver: CAUT/ Clarke Irwin, 1977) ; Margaret Gillett, *We Walked Very Warily: A History of Women at McGill* (Montreal: Eden Press, 1981); Mary Kinnear, "Discourse by Default: Women University Teachers," *In Subordination: Professional Women 1870-1970* (Montreal and Kingston: McGill-Queen's University Press, 1995); Alison Prentice, "Bluestockings, Feminists, or Women Workers? A Preliminary Look at Women's Early Employment at the University of Toronto," *Journal of the Canadian Historical Association* 2 (1991).

 3 Fingard, 691-3.

 4 DUA, MS1-3-A544, President's Office, Correspondence, vol. 19, Political Science 1922-47, R.A. MacKay to A.E. Kerr, 9 September 1946; Kerr to MacKay, 13 September 1946 (copy).

 5 University of British Columbia Archives, Board of Governors, Minutes, vol. 21, meeting of 21 December 1942; vol. 24, meetings of 30 April 1945 and 30 July 1945; interview with Robert M. Clark, Vancouver, BC, April 1987.

 6 John Norris, "Margaret Ormsby," *BC Studies* 32 (1976-7).

 7 P.B. Waite, *Lord of Point Grey: Larry MacKenzie of UBC* (Vancouver: UBC press, 1987), 142.

 8 Kathleen Coburn, *In Pursuit of Coleridge* (London, Toronto: Bodley Head, 1977), 58-9.

 9 David R. Murray and Robert A. Murray, *The Prairie Builder: Walter Murray of Saskatchewan* (Edmonton: NeWest Press,1984), 237.

10 James M. Pitsula, *An Act of Faith: The Early Years of Regina College* (Regina: Canadian Plains Research Center, University of Regina, 1988), 152; Michael Hayden, "A Short Biography of Hilda Neatby," in *So Much to Do, So Little Time: The Writings of Hilda Neatby*, ed. Michael Hayden (Vancouver: UBC Press, 1983), 25.

11 Michael Hayden to the author, 21 August 1995; "Interim Report of the CAUT Committee to Study the Extent of Discrimination against Women University Teachers," *CAUT Bulletin* 15 (1966).

12 Quoted in Robert Bothwell, *Laying the Foundation: A Century of History at the University of Toronto* (Toronto: Department of History, University of Toronto, 1991), 130.

13 Jill Ker Conway, *True North: A Memoir* (New York: Knopf, 1994), 122-4, 163-6.

14 Jean Burnet, "Minorities I Have Belonged To," *Canadian Ethnic Studies* 13 (1981): 30, 32.

15 Stanley Brice Frost, *McGill University, 1801-1895*, vol. 1 (Kingston and Montreal: McGill-Queen's University Press, 1980), 118, 158.

16 Flavelle quoted in Michael Bliss, *A Canadian Millionaire: The Life and Business Times of Sir Joseph Flavelle, Bart. 1858-1939* (Toronto: Macmillan, 1978), 203.

17 F.W. Gibson, *Queen's University, 1917-1961*, vol. 2 (Kingston and Montreal: McGill-Queen's University Press, 1983), 199-202; Stanley Brice Frost, *McGill University, 1985-1971*, vol. 2 (Kingston and Montreal: McGill-Queen's University Press, 1984), 128, 137, note 19; A.B. McKillop, *Matters of Mind* (Toronto: University of Toronto Press, 1994), 359-61; Bothwell, 68, 110; T. Moore, "Quota's End," *Manitoba Medicine* 59 (1989): 29-31; National Archives of Canada, MG 30, D204, F.H. Underhill Papers, vol. 4, Marvin Gelber to Underhill, 27 July 1936; University of Toronto Archives, President's Office (Cody), A68-0006/046(03), W.P.M. Kennedy to H.J. Cody, 21 Sept. 1940; conversation with Sydney Eisen, Toronto, August 1995; interview with Ernest Sirluck, Toronto, September 1995.

18 Sirluck interview, Toronto, September 1995; Ernest Sirluck, *First Generation, An Autobiography* (Toronto: University of Toronto Press, 1996), 30-98 passim; interview with Albert Rose, Toronto, November 1995.

19 Sirluck interview, Toronto, September 1995; Sirluck, 154-5.

20 Herbert A. Strauss and Werner Roder, eds., *International Biographical Dictionary of Central European Emigres 1993-1945, Vol. 2: The Arts, Sciences and Literature* (München, New York, London, Paris: Research Foundation for Jewish Immigration, New York, and Institut für Zeitgeschichte München, 1983), passim; Lawrence D. Stokes, "Canada and an Academic Refugee from Nazi Germany: The Case of Gerhard Herzberg," *Canadian Historical Review* 57 (1976): 151-3.

21 McGill University Archives, Principal's Office, RG2, c.47/442, memorandum for Principal Douglas, 7 July 1938.

22 Ibid., T. H. Matthews to Lewis Douglas, 24 January 1939; Douglas to Matthews, 26 January 1939 (copy).

23  Gerald E. Dirks, *Canada's Refugee Policy: Indifference or Opportunism?* (Montreal and London: McGill-Queen's University Press, 1977), 50-71; Irving Abella and Harold Troper, *None Is Too Many: Canada and the Jews of Europe 1933-1948* (Toronto: Lester and Orpen Dennys, 1982), 38-66; G.F.G. Stanley, cited in Abella and Troper, "Canada and the Refugee Intellectual, 1933-1939," in *The Muses Flee Hitler; Cultural Transfer and Adaptation 1930-1945,* ed. Jarrell C. Jackman and Carole S. Borden (Washington, DC: Smithsonian Institution Press, 1983), 260.
24  Conversations with Jean Burnet, Toronto, November 1995, and Frances Henry, Toronto, December 1995.
25  Harry Con, Ronald J. Con, Graham Johnson, Edgar Wickberg, and William E. Willmott, *From China to Canada: A History of the Chinese Communities in Canada* (Toronto: McClelland & Stewart, 1982); Anthony B. Chan, *Gold Mountain: The Chinese in New World* (Vancouver: New Star Books, 1983); Ken Adachi, *The Enemy That Never Was: A History of the Japanese Canadians* (Toronto: McClelland & Stewart, 1976).

# 7
# Inclusion and the Academy: Debating a Good Idea Freely
*Judy Rebick*

Certainly, universities should reach out, but people should also reach in and not enough people do that. I am somebody who reached into the university from the outside. I taught at the University of Regina a few years ago and now teach at the University of Toronto. I want to start by sharing some of my perceptions.

I was surprised by a number of things when I started teaching at the University of Regina, and I want to tell you about the three things that surprised me most. The first was the incredible autonomy that professors have. When I came to the university, I had never taught a class and had no academic qualifications. But no one said anything to me about what I should teach. Nobody observed me teaching, and nobody asked what I was going to teach. If I hadn't asked for help, I could have walked into that classroom with no preparation in political science and taught whatever I wanted to. I found this fact extraordinary. I have worked in many different places in my life, and I had never run into anything like that. I was shocked by it. I found out that no one ever observed anyone's class. What was called collegiality wasn't about helping each other or supporting each other. I'm still not sure what collegiality means. And I think this extreme autonomy that professors have is part of the problem on campus today.

The second thing that surprised me was that the men in the class talked much more than the women. I was surprised by this fact, because it was 1993 and because I was the teacher, which I thought might have intimidated some of the young men at first. It took work on my part, especially in public policy class, to get the women to talk.

The third thing that surprised me was the thin skin of my colleagues. This fact astonished me because I always thought of universities as the place for a clash of ideas, the place for debate. It was why I wanted a year at a university: to have discussion and debate.

I didn't find as much as I expected, and I wrote about my disappointment for a women's studies newsletter. Some people at the University of Regina won't talk to me anymore because I wrote that article, and many more were angry with me. Things also became hyperpolarized in the department over a serious dispute about hiring. This dispute had nothing to do with gender, but it got so bitter people stopped talking. We even had to have two events to say goodbye to me because they wouldn't sit at the same table. These three observations about my experience at the University of Regina, which ◦ I suspect is not so different from other campuses, shed some light on this discussion of why the university is having such a hard time coping with changes that so obviously have to be made.

I graduated from McGill University in 1967, a few years after that institution eliminated the quota for Jews. When I went to university, I did not have a single female professor in four years. Not one. I studied one book written by a woman, *Middlemarch* by George Eliot, a woman with a man's name because she couldn't get published as a woman. I was part of the surge of women on campus. By then, women were 37 percent of the student population. If you think about that – no women professors (there were a handful of women professors at McGill University, I just didn't happen to have any of them), no books by women – you realize how dramatically things have changed in thirty years. From the point of view of women's participation, it is a stunning, positively revolutionary change. We also have this massive change in our culture in terms of the participation of Aboriginal people and people of colour who have immigrated to our country and who have had access to postsecondary education at a much greater rate. Just before I entered university, there was a massive expansion of postsecondary education, which meant that working-class kids had access to postsecondary education in a way that ten years before wasn't even dreamed about.

So in the last generation, there have been massive changes in society and on campus. People who think that things can just go on as they always have, given that kind of change, are kidding themselves. It is not rational to think that you can have such change in the members of the academy and still keep running the university in the same way. It is just not possible. Peter Gzowski said it well. He was being interviewed for a documentary about Doris Anderson, who is a pioneer feminist in this country. She used to be the editor of *Chatelaine* in the 1960s, when it was a feminist magazine. Doris was an excellent editor. She increased *Chatelaine*'s circulation from 600,000 to 1.5 million by writing about feminist issues and speaking to a generation of women who were starting to feel something was wrong with their lives and were reading about their concerns in *Chatelaine*. When the job of editing *Maclean's* magazine opened up, Doris applied. Peter Gzowski also applied. Peter said in this interview, "It is not that I am underplaying my qualifications, but there is no question that Doris was more qualified than I was, and I was hired because I was a man." And then he said, "You have to realize that in those days you know, it was really a boys' club," and he smiled because he was thinking about it. "If you were a guy it was really comfortable then, but it wasn't fair, it wasn't fair." It was a wonderful insight.

It isn't easy to change when things are great for you. It isn't easy to see the need for change. On campus, men have found it hard to see the need for change, just as some white women have found it hard to see the need to open up the women's movement to women of colour. When you are in the dominant group, when things are good for you, when things feel comfortable for you, you just assume that it is good for everyone. I don't know why it is so hard to understand that someone else's reality can be different from your reality. (An old African proverb says, "As long as lions don't have historians, the history of the hunt will always celebrate the hunter.") I am amazed by the number of people on the other side of this debate who refuse to recognize the simple truth that those with power, even relative power, experience reality in a different way than those with less power.

The second thing I want to talk about is why universities have such a hard time changing. Universities were one of the first places where women started to make gains, so why are they so much more resistant to change than many other institutions? Part of the problem is this notion that academic freedom means you can do whatever you want in your classroom and nobody can say anything about it. I don't think that is academic freedom. Academic freedom is about freedom of inquiry. It should not be about freedom to say anything you please, no matter who is hurt. Academic freedom should not protect Professor Yaqzan in New Brunswick who says that date rape is natural behaviour for young men.

Many men find offensive the claim that the academy was created by men for men. But this statement is a fact. It's not a value judgment. Men created an institution where they could feel comfortable and operate at their maximum potential, which makes sense. But when women came into that institution, it had to change so that women could operate at their full potential. That is common sense.

Part of the resistance to change is the extreme individualism in the academy. In some institutions, such as the Ontario Institute for Studies in Education, there is an attempt to make professors more accountable for what happens in the classroom. Critics of such programs are apt to say that sensitivity training or classes in antisexism, antiracism, or crosscultural communication somehow interfere with academic freedom. How can learning new ideas interfere with academic freedom? I don't get that. Just as I don't understand how judges taking sensitivity training on sexism and racism interferes with judicial independence. Learning new ideas does not challenge independence. If learning new ideas changes your mind, isn't that a good thing? I debate people with different ideas from mine every day. I believe in debate. The clash of ideas is at the heart of democracy and education. But I don't see much clashing in academia.

Most students I know don't feel that they can express their ideas freely in the classroom. They feel they have to say what the professor thinks or they won't get good marks. When we have a clash of ideas, it very quickly gets polarized and antagonistic.

Now I want to talk about why I think "chilly climate" discussions have become so polarized and hostile. Every situation I've looked at where this issue of chilly climate becomes hot seems to have a common characteristic: one or more men in the department are accused of harassment, and other men in the department cover up for them or are silent. If a professor is accused of sexual or racial harassment, there should be formal charges against that person. Those men who are harassing students or other faculty should be held accountable on the one hand and have due process to answer such charges on the other.

But most "chilly climate" issues are not about harassment. They are issues about male culture. They are issues about marginalization, which is not the same as harassment, and issues of marginalization should not be dealt with by judicial procedures or quasi-judicial procedures. They should be dealt with by discussion, debate, education, and the introduction of new pedagogical techniques.

But what happens is these two issues get confused. Often when students try to raise complaints about chilly climate – not about harassment, but about feeling marginalized, feeling trivialized, feeling undervalued, feeling their ideas aren't heard – they are asked for proof. They are told, "How you feel is not evidence."

Do you need to go into a court of law to prove that you are marginalized? If someone who is silent in class feels marginalized, and more than one person feels that way, and they all happen to be black, or they happen to be women, that perception is a reality. It is not appropriate to have to prove the point in a court of law. If the women in a university department feel they are marginalized, it is not a question of whose fault it is, and the solution is not through the sexual harassment office. But it is still a problem that needs a solution, and it seems to me that we should be able to solve it.

In this debate, I find an assumption that academic freedom is a more important value than inclusion. I don't accept that assumption. But I also don't accept the assumption that in every situation, inclusion is more important than academic freedom. For example, there is a conflict in the Rushton case, and any discussion of the Bell curve (here, related to the idea that blacks are less intelligent than whites) in class creates such a conflict. When conflicts like these do happen, then we need to look at them and say where is the greater harm. That is what the court does when there is a conflict of rights: it looks at where the greater harm would be done and balances the rights to minimize harm. That is what we have to do when academic freedom and inclusion conflict.

Context is important in deciding this balance. David Suzuki has argued that we shouldn't be able to put forward ideas like Rushton's. I am not sure I agree with Dr. Suzuki, but I do agree that context is essential. This summer I saw *Merchant of Venice* at Stratford. I had never seen the play before, and I was shocked by its anti-Semitism. There is no question in my mind that the play is valuable and should be performed, but I would not have felt the same way about its performance in Germany during the Second World War. And so the idea of context is important when we balance academic freedom and the inclusive university. If students feel marginalized, then issues like racism are much more charged than if students feel included. That is a valid consideration for a university or any other institution.

Many academics claim that they are terrified to say anything in their classes for fear of being accused of racism or sexism. It's not very pleasant to be accused of racism or sexism. It is very uncomfortable. I have been accused of racism, and I didn't like it, but it did not stop me from saying what I think. It did make me think about whether what I said was racist. An accusation of racism or sexism does not interfere with academic freedom. Academic freedom doesn't mean being free from criticism, even nasty criticism. Everywhere in society when you say something unpopular, you suffer consequences. Academic freedom means you shouldn't lose your job for having an unpopular opinion, but it doesn't shield you from criticism or even attack. Now if legions of professors were being accused unfairly of racial or sexual harassment, then I could see a problem. But even after years of this debate, there is no evidence that these legions exist.

Some opponents of inclusion appear to believe that equality-seeking groups started asserting their rights only after the Charter. I find this a curious perception. The Charter came into force in 1985. I date the rise of the second wave of the women's movement back to the late 1960s or early 1970s, and certainly women had been agitating on campus since the early 1970s.

What happened with the Charter is not that people started agitating but rather that the power relations changed. The agitation got some legal backup in 1985. I heard a political science professor at the Learneds say that a university professor has no power. It is certainly true that a university professor doesn't have as much power as the prime minister of a country or the president of a university. But in the classroom, the university professor has all the power. Students want good marks, and the professor has the power to give them good marks. That is power. Students don't feel able to challenge the professor until the professor gives them permission to do so. And this situation is especially true for students who feel marginalized. So there has to be a mechanism for students to complain if they are upset about something the professor has done or said, or about how the department operates. If we want to have an inclusive university, if we don't want silenced students to drop out, there has to be a mechanism. Maybe an ombudsperson. I don't think that person should be the sexual harassment officer, unless actual harassment is involved.

Some of you might not agree that women need a different learning environment than men. I was resistant to this idea, but I am learning otherwise. One example of how much more men feel empowered to talk comes from my experience hosting *Face Off*. Our television audience was equally divided between men and women. We had a contest where we invited viewers to write to us about the record of the Chrétien government and win a seat at the *Face Off* debating table. Ninety people submitted entries. How many women do you think applied? Two. Two women. I was shocked. I then realized *Face Off* is an ideal speech situation, but it is not a very female speech situation. Most women wouldn't feel comfortable with all that competitive, aggressive debate. So if *Face Off* represents the kind of atmosphere you have in your class, most women are unlikely to participate.

I have also felt for some time that learning how to teach is a very important part of getting rid of this chilly climate. Learning how to teach better and to be more inclusive, using techniques to include quiet people and discourage those who dominate discussion, could be just as important as antiracism and antisexism. Clearer departmental communication and accountability would also help. And we already know from the women's movement that informal mechanisms often exclude those who are marginalized.

My last story is about one of my students, a South Asian woman born in Canada. In class, we were discussing racism, and she told this story:

I am the only woman of colour skydiving instructor in Canada, and I have been working with a group of white men and one white woman for four years. One day in my class, I said, "I think it is a problem that we don't have more women and more people of colour skydiving. I think we should outreach, maybe even have some kind of affirmative action program to encourage women and people of colour to skydive." Suddenly these men, not all of them, turned on me and said, "That would be reverse discrimination. Why did you have to raise that?" They got really angry at me, and after that they changed the way they related to me. The other woman didn't say anything.

So my student was upset, and later she asked the white woman, "Why didn't you say anything?" The white woman said, "If I said anything, they would have hated me, too."

This story illustrates very well what it takes to be antiracist. People of colour don't have a choice. They have to deal with racism in their lives. But if you are white, you don't have to deal with racism in your life unless you choose to. My student's friend chose not to stand up to the attack on her. The other men also remained silent. And it is the same with sexism. If you are a man, you don't have to deal with sexism in your life unless you choose to. Gender polarization doesn't happen unless you side with your gender.

I have seen this behaviour more often than I like to admit: men siding with each other because one man is accused of sexism. But when you are in solidarity with the man doing wrong rather than with the woman who is seeking change, then you are part of the problem. One of the good phrases we had in the sixties was "If you're not part of the solution, you're part of the problem." And that is true when we deal with racism and sexism. If you are in the dominant group, you must work hard to be part of the solution.

My metaphor for diversity is a symphony. And in this symphony everyone has to play well, but everyone also has to listen to the other instruments. Unless they do both – play well and listen – then they don't have a beautiful symphony; they have discordance. And if the symphony were just the violins playing all the time, and you couldn't hear the brass and you couldn't hear the woodwinds, it would get tiresome. It wouldn't be as rich; it wouldn't be as beautiful. And that is what our society has been. I don't know if you want to think of men as violins, but we have heard one section of the orchestra for centuries. Now, the other sections of the orchestra are playing, and they are good. Make room to hear them, too. It is not easy to do, but if we can do it, then the results will be spectacular. I look forward to that performance.

# 8
# Academic Freedom and Its Distractions
*Stan Persky*

My focus is on some misleading educational developments, coming from allegedly diametrically opposite political directions. I think they will seriously further erode what Peter Emberley calls in *Zero Tolerance* "the scholarly culture" and "its two predominant animating principles – reading in the tradition of books and renewal by conversations." And I believe that the long-run threat to academic freedom emanating from the marketplace demand that the universities see themselves as "engines of economic growth" and "job-training centres" is greater than the other dangers to be contemplated; namely, those of behaviour and speech codes, or harassment policies, and the spectre and/or promise of new teaching machines.

Although the focus of my attention will primarily be on internal ideological and technological distractions, I want to make sure that I acknowledge, as a larger framework, the tendency of the economy to subsume politics, of entertainment to replace art, and of entrepreneurial schemes to diminish liberal education, even while pretending to save it. Because it's characteristic in dark musings of this sort to subject readers to considerable formal exposition and theoretical formulations, I'll attempt, in the name of discursive relief, to uphold the genre of the shaggy dog story. So, first, let me say a few things about entrepreneurial colleges, computer panaceas, and campus therapy, before closing with some observations about academic freedom as a democratic power.

A senior administrator at my college – a very nice person, committed to liberal education, sensible, decent, and so on – turned up recently to talk to the faculty members of my division and tell us what our college was up to. The big idea, he quickly revealed, was entrepreneurial education – revenue-generating projects that would increase the institution's fiscal independence, affording us relief from the budgetary whims of passing provincial governments. The first of these projects under exploration, he announced, was

China. I must admit that I missed the economic details of this proposal, other than that it was financially favourable to us. Apparently, someone in China was starting up one or more private postsecondary institutions and was seeking some sort of business and intellectual partnership with a North American institution that would provide curriculum and faculty.

Indeed, my attention was so adrift that I didn't really wake up until our administrator said, "And so, you would have the choice of teaching on either the Lynnmour campus or the China campus." I'm pretty sure he didn't name some city in China, like Beijing or Shanghai. He just said, "China." Now, I should mention that my college is a minuscule provincial institution tucked into a patch of woods on the first ridge of hills on the north shore of suburban Vancouver. What got my attention was what seemed like a comical category mistake; namely, the equation of "Lynnmour campus," located in the bucolic Lynn Valley of British Columbia, and the entire nation of China. He made it sound so easy: Lynnmour – China. Take your pick. Whichever you like.

While I was still figuring out what possible discourse would permit these two items to be fit into a single category of some virtual geography exercise, our intrepid entrepreneurial administrator had already moved on to the next project: We've had an inquiry to mount business management programs in Lebanon. Again, I was nonplussed. Most of us had come to this meeting thinking about things on the order of "Gee, I wonder if we can get a couple of extra ten-thirty teaching time-slots in next semester's schedule now that the new building has opened." Instead: Lebanon wants our business management programs.

Our visionary was unfazed. The first lady of Panama, he reported, wants to establish a "city of knowledge" – a vast educational complex with students from around the world that would be housed in former, now abandoned, American military bases in that Central American country. And again, I found myself about three steps behind, as I had been all through this recital. While he was onto the military bases question, I was still thinking to myself, "The first lady of Panama? There's a first lady of Panama? And she wants a 'city of knowledge'? What next?"

I didn't have long to wonder. "What next" was the West Coast Express. Only a few loose ends remained to be tied up on the West Coast Express deal, we were assured. Once it was "in place," teachers from our college would apparently be offering courses to early morning commuters travelling the West Coast Express train from the suburb of Maple Ridge to their downtown Vancouver office jobs. We already know, our administrator said – I can barely convey the tone of chipper good will and enthusiasm in which all of this was told to us – what courses the commuters want on the way in to work – accounting, and spreadsheets, or something – but the one detail to be nailed down was that we weren't sure, from the surveys and focus groups that we'd done, just exactly what courses the commuters wanted on the ride home to Maple Ridge.

While you're contemplating the possibilities of music appreciation courses and/or bedtime stories as the commuter train goes clackety-clacking toward the horizon of Maple Ridge and beyond, let me pause in this true tale – although I realize it sounds like something from a wicked satirical novel about academia – to note that it was at that moment I began to understand, for the first time, the dimensions of the phrase "inclusive university." If the administrators at my little backwater – but excellent – arts and sciences college are contemplating such ventures and calling it education, what sorts of deals do you suppose the CEO's of major educational enterprises are negotiating? The moral of the story is: It might be possible and profitable to manufacture widgets at postsecondary institutions, but why call it education? Why not call it a widget factory?

I want to discuss computers in the fewest possible sentences because I know that everyone in the field of education already knows all about them and their growing place in whatever institution they're working at. I'll therefore spare us a disquisition on what the full-scale entry of computers in education and the arrival of the legion of technical attendants they require for their maintenance is doing to university budgets. I'll refrain from indulging in the debate about their vital or not-so-vital role in pedagogy. Indeed, I want to offer little more than a definition and a commonsense observation.

The commonsense observation is that computers are a tool and, if a tool is useful to the task at hand, use it. Of course, as we know from Benjamin Barber's *Jihad vs. McWorld*, it's not quite as simple as that, because the matching of tools and needs is not only a natural process, but rather needs are often created as addictively felt wants, and technologies become imperative rather than optional.

In the larger view, the computer is the latest solution to a classic dream. Sometimes, the dream is called the perpetual motion machine, or the philosopher's stone, or the alchemist's formula to transmute lead into gold. At times, all of the versions of the dream seem like blasphemies on the original vision of the transubstantiation of wine and bread into blood and flesh. In this case, the dream is that of the great teaching machine. Of course, those of us who practise the teaching arts have already been through this once in our careers when that great oxymoron, educational television, was offered up as a surefire panacea. A quarter-century later the main function of educational television, as we know, is its use in the *second* amphitheatre where herds of students have been sequestered because the first amphitheatre where the prof is lecturing live is already full; I'm sure there are surveys showing that the students in the second amphitheatre are happier watching the lecture next door on a giant TV screen than the students in the first amphitheatre who have to watch the insect-sized lecturer down in the pit. In many institutions, a similar screen has now been installed in the first amphitheatre, and the students there are now able to ignore the live lecturer entirely in favour of the warm and fuzzy feelings that television apparently produces. And naturally, no one wants to discuss whether it's a good educational idea for two amphitheatres full of undergraduates to be "taking" – I use that word advisedly – such courses.

I've no idea if computers will achieve comparable success. I suppose so. But the main thing to remember is that the new teaching machine, philosopher's stone, lead-into-gold formula, appeals to two temptations. First, there's the teacher's temptation to get out of teaching, and second, there's the administration's temptation to get rid of teaching. This situation is, as one of my mentors often said, another error whose time has come.

As for myself, I've been developing a method I call nonalgorithmic teaching. This is a pedagogy that reduces the need for in-class technology and is designed to be resistant to reproduction or simulation by computer. So far, I've managed to get rid of classroom television, slideshows, dancing dog demonstrations, overhead projectors and, a couple of years ago, I even gave up that ultimate technology that stands between us and the abyss of silence, namely, chalk. Now, I just sit there and we talk.

Finally, in terms of the distractions, here are some extended thoughts about various subtopics I'll put under the rubric of "therapy."

About four or five years ago, I more or less innocently attended the faculty union meeting at my college at which the subject of sexual harassment was introduced as an issue for consideration. I say "innocently attended" because although I had followed and participated in the debates launched by the women's movement over the last quarter-century and had read all the major texts in the field, I see retrospectively that I was, for a variety of reasons – some social and some personal – something of an innocent about what was at issue. This innocence may be a sort of occupational hazard to which people who teach philosophy are especially prone.

In any case, I was prepared to enter the discussion with the requisite inquiring temperament and a willingness to seek actual remedies. When the issue of sexual harassment was called to my attention, my initial (and continuing) response was that, of course, we ought to do something to prevent it. I had little idea of the possible extent of sexually harassing behaviour at the institution where I taught, but I was assured by various colleagues that it was significant enough to deserve specific attention.

There were, I was told, frequent acts of repeated unwanted sexual touching or fondling, threatening demands for sexual favours, and proposals of rewards in exchange for sex – what was once known in academia as an "A

for a lay." I was (and remain) prepared to hold up my hand at the appropriate time to vote for the resolution to stop this sort of thing.

Well, the appropriate time and the resolution soon appeared. Except that
there was something very curious about the resolution. Before I say what
was curious about the resolution – and it was, I should note, a resolution
that was to be inserted into the legal contract between the college and its
teachers – let me make a couple of remarks.

First, there already existed an extensive process of monitoring and evaluating the performance and behaviour of teachers, which included the acts
now called "sexual harassment," and included sanctions such as reprimands,
suspensions, and even firing. There was a nice old-fashioned phrase for that
sort of thing. It was called, back in the nineteen fifties and sixties, "moral
turpitude," and we all rather savoured the word "turpitude," bemused by
what it might exactly mean. In any case, it was eventually succeeded by the
clearly more antiseptic phrase, "termination for just cause." Furthermore,
there already existed a squad of counsellors, division coordinators, deans,
vice presidents, and sundry other administrators, with whom one might
lodge complaints.

Second, and in addition to this considerable machinery, there was the
question of intellectual climate. Our college was one of the leading sites
where a critique of sexism, racism, homophobia, and various other discrimi-
nations had been developed. There was not only a critique but also widespread advocacy, among the teachers, of values designed to undercut such
sexism, racism, homophobia, and so on. Now, a lot of people who aren't
particularly fond of academic institutions like to pretend not only that such
institutions didn't lead the way in exploring these issues but also that they
are among the prime offenders. No one has demonstrated that either claim
has any empirical weight, but they're still frequently heard, often from academics themselves.

Despite this context of available mechanisms of remedy and intellectual
advocacy against discriminatory behaviours, I was willing to support specific action against sexual harassment, on the grounds of collegiality and
with the thought in mind that there were some acts, lying between Criminal Code offences and institutional regulatory codes, that might be captured by such a policy in such a way that would be an improvement on
existing methods. Then came the proposed policy. I'll quote the crucial
curious section, although members of similar institutions will be familiar
with the wording. It says: "Sexual harassment is comment or conduct of a
sexual nature, including sexual advances, requests for sexual favours, sug-
gestive comments or gestures, or physical contact when any one of the following occurs: a) the conduct is engaged in, or the comment is made, by a
person who knows, or ought reasonably to know, that the conduct or comment is unwanted or unwelcome; b) the conduct or comment has the effect

of creating an intimidating, hostile or offensive environment, and may include the expression of sexist attitudes, language and behaviour." This wording was followed by several other clauses that referred to illicit rewards, reprisals, threats, and so on.

The fact that the policy was written in execrably convoluted prose that was grammatically suspect wasn't curious. I understand what committees are capable of doing to language. Anyway, when I asked why it was so badly written and reasoned, I was assured by a committee member that "we merely copied the wording from the University of British Columbia's policy." I winced at this confession of plagiarism but decided to pass. I was more concerned about reasoning. If one parsed the policy, it said, among many other things, "Sexual harassment is comment of a sexual nature when the comment has the effect of creating an offensive [classroom] environment, and it may include the expression of sexist attitudes."

Clearly, we were a long way from the acts that I thought we were trying to prevent. Indeed, it seemed to me that acts and mere words had been conflated by the proposed policy. By "mere words" I mean words that aren't acts, such as, say, threats. Worse, the conflation of acts and words depended on ambiguous, undefined phrases that would be left for interpretation to the administrators of the complicated quasi-judicial procedures that the policy's drafters envisaged. Among those phrases are "of a sexual nature," "offensive environment," and "sexist attitudes."

I wanted to know if an utterance, delivered in the classroom, to the effect that pornography is mere free expression protected by the Constitution and that a once-current slogan, "Porn is the theory, rape is the practice," is intellectually imbecilic, qualified under the proposed policy. Were remarks about pornography "of a sexual nature"? Was the sentiment uttered one that could create an "offensive environment"? Did the forceful rejection of a well-known maxim of antipornography feminists in itself constitute a "sexist attitude"? The answer to all of those questions, lamentably, is, a resounding yes. Of course, my colleagues at the union meeting assured me that the answers were no and, to placate me and to assuage my concerns, a phrase, probably also copied from UBC's policy, was inserted to assure us that the "policy is not intended to infringe upon the ability of instructors to academically discuss issues of harassment, sexism and sexuality."

To end this anecdote, what had happened was that somebody's idea of sexism and how to eradicate it was imported into a policy purportedly meant to prevent acts of sexual harassment. The levels of duplicity, misguided sincerity, and sandbox power politics involved in all of this can be passed over.

Intended or not, it seems to me that there is a conflation of acts and words in this policy, and the policy endangers the utterance of some words at a place, ironically, that is a privileged site for free speech. Furthermore, that speech is protected by a law that trumps local regulatory policy, namely, section 2 of the Canadian Charter of Rights and Freedoms. There's a complicated bit of law involved here, which I won't explicate, but it is the case that colleges, if not universities, are in law, "emanations of government" and therefore subject to the Charter. Eventually, someone will notice this fact and charge the college with a violation of the Constitution or will simply go to an appropriate court and seek a constitutional ruling.

Once we established the sexual harassment policy and instituted the mechanisms for sexual harassment procedures, including securing a sexual harassment officer ideologically committed to the particular view of harassment implicit in the policy, we then embarked on an expansionary policy discussion that has dragged on at my school for several years, although at most other schools is apparently a settled issue.

The logic of the expanded policy discussion went like this: If it is recognized that there can be sexual harassment of the type defined, then what about harassment directed at various groups of people who are specifically protected against discrimination by human rights legislation? What about racial, homophobic, religious, and disability-related forms of harassment? Of course, as I've already noted, few things are more powerful at an academic institution than a bad idea whose time has come, or perhaps we should say, a punishment whose crime has come.

Although I understood at least part of the sexual harassment policy and could see the point of preventing particular acts, the new proposal struck me as puzzling. When I asked if there were significant numbers of incidents of professors racially or homophobically harassing students and/or each other, there were dark mutterings but absolutely nothing that resembled empirical evidence. When I asked what acts this proposed policy would address that were not already addressed by existing mechanisms, there was no satisfactory reply.

I don't mean to sound unduly cynical, but given the absence of good reasons for having this policy, a committee was naturally brought into being. The committee duly laboured over the proposed new policy. Eventually, the faculty representative to the committee returned to the faculty to ask us to vote on draft number seven of the proposed policy. I barely paused to imagine the amount of time and number of meetings that must have been required to get to draft number seven.

The crucial clause in the new policy, which became known around our institution as the "have a nice day clause," read: "Personal harassment is ... unwelcome behaviour or comment that is directed at or is offensive to any person within the college community by any person who knows, or ought reasonably to know, that the behaviour or comment demeans, belittles, or causes personal humiliation or embarrassment to that person." There were various other clauses in the policy, but this one was the clause that led a faculty member to suggest that any comment beyond "Have a nice day" might be grounds for complaint.

Our faculty rejected this proposal abjuring us to be nice or else and, ever since, various parties have sought to craft a policy that the faculty would accept. The issue was only recently resolved at my school. Unable to devise a policy that the faculty could agree to, our union executive proposed a motion that the faculty commit itself to the principle of creating a personal harassment policy and that we'd figure out the content of the policy later on. I hope the logical absurdity of this proposal is evident because I despair of explaining it. Almost predictably, a plurality of the faculty voted in favour of the principle, and a new committee was struck to craft the policy. Opponents of the policy were now formally restricted from opposing the principle of the policy and could only propose amendments to the eventual wording of the proposed policy. Even this process was abandoned, and the whole thing was removed from faculty's hands and turned over to the provincial instructors' association for a ready-made solution.

Before concluding this cautionary tale, let me also direct a word to those whose hyperbole inclines them to think that harassment policies and other therapeutic measures are the greatest academic disaster of the fin de siècle. They aren't. It's important to distinguish between enemies and distractions. Harassment policies, speech codes, and the popular ideology of therapeutically treating the "whole student" and even his or her "inner student" strike me as a distraction, not a destruction of the entire educational enterprise.

Let me also say a word to those who are offended by any criticism whatsoever of such policies and who are overly quick to spot a backlash of ancient sexists, racists, and homophobes once more raising their ugly heads (and other parts of their anatomies). My word is this: If you can't persuade someone who is fundamentally disposed toward such policies that the excesses of the policy need to be reined in, I don't see how you're going to conquer the hordes of old-and-new fogies who will turn backlash into self-fulfilling prophecy.

Let me conclude with some recommendations for remedy: first, the existing harassment policy should be scaled back to capture identifiable acts rather than extended into a blanket personal harassment policy. Second, most of the words that such policies attempt to silence and sanction should be left to the public forum for debate. Third, if we're to have quasi-adjudicating special harassment personnel rather than leaving this responsibility to administrators, then criteria ought to be established to minimize the possibility of the office being occupied by persons who are clearly partisan advocates for the particular ideological reading of the policy that does constitute a danger to academic freedom. The reason that the speech code debate has captured such a significant degree of academic attention is that many faculty accurately sense a larger ideological agenda at work than the eradication of acts of harassment. They sense, accurately, an effort to mandate a curriculum that seriously infringes on what up to now have been understood as the parameters of "academic freedom."

Let me immediately add, however, that academic freedom has never been understood as an absolute freedom; it has always been constrained by concepts of "teaching competence" and "professional conduct," and some of the objectionable behaviours that harassment policies aim at are legitimately within the arc of those concepts. But, as I've noted, the tendency of such policies to conflate that which is objectionable from anyone's human rights perspective with that which ought to be strictly under the purview of the teachers has created a need to more clearly explain academic freedom.

There are many views on offer of what academic freedom might be. One of the better-known postmodern neopragmatists, Stanley Fish of the University of Illinois at Chicago, the author of a book extravagantly called *There's No Such Thing as Free Speech ... And It's a Good Thing, Too,* has lately discovered that liberalism is an ideology rather than the neutral cipher it sometimes purports to be.

Liberalism, as an inclusive doctrine of toleration, it turns out, is itself intolerant of those who are themselves terminally intolerant. The inclusive university, Dr. Fish discovers, is a chimera; liberalism is a lie, and it's time, in his view, for plain talk. "The assertion of interest is always what's going on," he says, "even when, and especially when, interest wraps itself in high-sounding abstractions ... Politics is all there is, and it's a good thing too. Principles and abstractions don't exist except as the rhetorical accompaniments of practices in search of good public relations."[1] Almost needless to add, in Dr. Fish's view, there's no such thing as academic freedom; there's only a power struggle, and by his lights, it's a good thing, too. This view is probably a more vulgar form of neopragmatism than was dreamed of by Richard Rorty, the modern promoter of such doctrines, but it may be an accurate derivation rather than a deviation.

In a more mainstream mode, Frederick Schauer, a constitutional law professor at Harvard who specializes in what's known as "conceptual clarification," offers the metaphor of an "exemption" or an "immunity" to capture the character of academic freedom. Schauer says that, conceptually, academic freedom is "an exemption from something that everyone else has to do," or alternatively, an immunity from, say, the proscription of certain utterances, a proscription applicable to everybody else.[2]

He then goes on to diminish this clarification further by noting that, in the United States, academic freedom "is not much of an issue" because First Amendment law in the United States protects everyone and allows everyone to say just about anything, so no special protection is required for academics. He allows that there's a slight difference in Canada; for instance, while utterances of holocaust denial are fully protected in the United States, statutory and case law in Canada indicate that utterances of holocaust denial are not protected, and therefore academics might need an exemption from such law to explore or engage in holocaust denial. All of this strikes me as disappointing. The metaphor of "exemption" seems ill-chosen to describe what is essentially a positive teaching power protected from improper intrusion by government and others.

The idea of the teaching power is most extensively discussed by Joseph Tussman in his 1977 book, *Government and the Mind,* and what he says there lays the groundwork for a meaningful conception of academic freedom. Tussman writes, "The teaching power is the inherent constitutional authority of the state to establish and direct the teaching activity and institutions needed to ensure its continuity and further its legitimate general and special purposes. It is rather strange that a governmental power so visible in its operation and so pervasive in effect should lack a familiar name." Tussman adds, "The teaching power is a peer to the legislative, the executive, and the judicial powers, if it is not, indeed, first among them."

In the broadest outline, here is how it's derived. In a democracy, power ought to reside with the people, who, in a constitution-making conclave, delegate certain of the day-to-day operations of that power to government. Furthermore, there is a "separation of powers" and "checks and balances" on that delegated power, based on the intuition that unseparated, unchecked delegated power will tend toward abuse and corruption. Thus, the legislative power is not to be abrogated by the executive power or the judicial power, and its independence is not to be intruded on by the other powers. As for the teaching power, we find it implicitly present in almost all constitutional documents – Tussman cites that of California, which says, "A general diffusion of knowledge and intelligence being essential to the preservation of the rights and liberties of the people, the legislature shall encourage by all suitable means the promotion of intellectual, scientific, moral and agricultural improvement." This position results in the web of offices and institutions in which the teaching power is invested.

I frequently joke with my students that, in addition to being a member of a global, transhistorical discipline, I'm also an officer of the Canadian state charged with the task of inculcating and interrogating the values, laws, and practices of Canadian democracy. I further argue that both of those functions, discipline and office, once appropriately vested through mechanisms of certification, appointment, and monitored performance, are protected from interference under the doctrine of the teaching power. That seems to me a tacit but logical feature of the division of powers in a democracy.

The teaching power deserves its degree of relative autonomy by virtue of its dual task, which is to inculcate citizenly virtues and to develop the critical thought at the heart of the deliberative practices of a democracy. Anything short of such a view of academic freedom trivializes the notion and probably renders it incomprehensible to the public. There's a great deal more to be said about academic freedom and how it's to be administered, but my immediate point is that such an idea of academic freedom only makes sense within a larger conception of forum democracy.

The notion of academic freedom is today often denigrated as objectionable licence or a sophistic cover for the protection of tenure. However, once academic freedom is conceived as a doctrine within the teaching power, such distractions ought to be dispelled. Whether or not the other aforementioned distractions are as easily cast aside, the concept of academic freedom acquires some added urgency, given our commitment to the "inclusive" university.

**Notes**
1   Stanley Fish, "What's Sauce for One Goose: The Logic of Academic Freedom," this volume, 11.
2   Frederick Schauer, "Academic Freedom: Rights as Immunities and Privileges," this volume, 13-14.  `

# Part 3
# Academic Freedom in Peril

# 9
# Academic Freedom versus the Intrusive University
*John Fekete*

"Civility" is frequently invoked in contexts of conflict in Canadian life, so much so that it almost seems to be a requirement for employment in Canadian universities. Canadians are almost always civil. In fact, Canada is a country as civil as you will find, and academics are just a little bit more civil than the rest of the country. So they always rush – especially in public – to reconciliation, to find common ground, to find ways of reaching agreement, to hide differences. Indeed, I have to draw your attention to the fact that the words "academic freedom *and* the inclusive university" offer up immediately the comforts of reconciliation. It is almost as though all of the controversy that you have been reading about in the newspapers and all the abuses of institutional power against ordinary working employees in universities were behind us or at least as though we were ready to put all of that behind us.

Certainly, that is something we would wish to see happen. I cannot, however, in good conscience say that we are at that point. Academic freedom *or* the inclusive university might be a more telling title. At a more modest, realistic level, you would at least have to say "academic freedom *versus* the inclusive university," just to keep the tension, the reality of conflict, under scrutiny. The preposition *versus* reminds us that many debates are ahead, and many more cries of distress, many more accommodations, many more conflicts and, unfortunately, perhaps many more abuses can be expected before we move on to some other territory of reform and conflict.

There is a political relationship between the practices of academic freedom and the practices associated with what some people call "the inclusive university." To be specific, academic freedom is under attack, and here and there, it is also being enacted and defended. The faculty's contractual prerogatives, not universally admired, but important nonetheless, are under attack. Both the corporate rights of peer process and the academic's rights of intellectual commitment have been coming under attack from government, from administrations, sometimes from students, and often from other members of faculty.

Universities have to be universities of academic freedom. This goal is a
defining attribute that arises from a continual struggle for its realization
throughout the history of universities. By contrast, what the current advocacy of "inclusion" means is yet to be defined. The experience of what is
called "inclusion" in the universities often seems to come in the form of
censorship or in the form of anti-intellectual pressure for change. To be
sure, "inclusion" is a concept that implies a continuation of the long revolution of democracy, the continuing opening of the university to people
who have not hitherto had a chance to participate in it. That is an important and positive process. At the same time, in any social process, we have
to be alert to possible abuses. The concept of "inclusion," once put into
practice, may not function as a natural process of democratization that can
be taken at face value as an extension of franchise, compatible with the
kind of life form that a university is. On the contrary, "inclusion" may also
serve as an alibi for an undesirable political moralism that self-righteously
selects some groups and some strands of ideas for preferential treatment
and actually degrades the pluralism of a democratic university to a narrowly selective orthodoxy.

In fact, as a description of the current trend in universities, the "inclusive
university" is a less appropriate term than "intrusive university." This intrusion is said to be on behalf of designated client groups consisting of members who are said to be vulnerable and/or disadvantaged. It is also an intrusion
on behalf of what are called the expectations of society or rather the demands for accountability in the fulfilment of social policy.

The commonsense meaning of "inclusion" has the genuine virtue of bringing democratic, energetic, and intellectual opportunities to the university.
From my point of view, the kinds of changes that have occurred in the
university over the last two decades – the demographic and intellectual
changes, the increasing attention to issues of feminism and multiculturalism,
the range of new philosophical and social/scientific intellectual programs,
and the methods we broadly call postmodern – have all made the university more interesting and more alive than it was when I began my own
undergraduate degree.

The dangers of intrusion are nonetheless there as well, and we have to do
some intellectual, historical, and moral housecleaning to separate inclusion from intrusion, because some of the intrusive forms of "inclusion"
pose a real risk of bureaucratic damage to the university as an institution
with its own defining properties. Let me explain what I mean by making a
few observations about the current discussions of academic freedom in the
university.

Contrary to what is often said, academic freedom is *not* a robust institution in our universities and our societies. It is sometimes said that academic
freedom could take some downgrading: after all, it is so powerful, everybody

agrees to it, nobody would ever question it. As researchers have pointed out, however, to a very considerable extent, Canadians take self-censorship for granted. Canadians are very constrained, very *civil,* and often all too ready to take into account the impact of the things they say before they say them.

More specifically, academic freedom in the modern sense is a relatively new institution. We owe it as a contractual right to the work of the Canadian Association of University Teachers, and that association did not really turn to the topic until the 1960s. Only one generation of professors has had academic freedom institutionalized fully in contracts and agreements between academic staff and universities. Academic freedom is not a simple concept; it includes different components touching on both the rights of academic peers as a group (that is, employment and professional rights within and outside the university) and the rights of individual academics. And academic freedom is not equally well defended in its different components.

By now, the privileges of the professions, of academics vis-à-vis employers and the external world, are reasonably well in place. But the protections for individuals within the professions and the universities are not nearly so strong. Academic freedom as a right has been won over many years *against* countervailing demands to establish a homogeneity of the intellect. In Canada, this homogeneity was articulated in terms of specific expectations of loyalty: to God, or Britain, or capitalism. At various times, dissenters from any one of these loyalties would find they had lost their jobs. To be sure, the universities had autonomy from government, but for a very long time, the universities did not extend that autonomy to the individuals within them. In fact, the university accommodated, often with the help of the professoriate, prevailing social pressures. Conformity has always been the wall against which academic freedom throws itself.

The same tends to be true in both Canada and the United States. During the First World War, the president of Columbia University made it absolutely clear that professors unable to espouse complete, enthusiastic, and patriotic support of the war effort would be unwelcome in the university. Similarly, in the 1930s, the leader of the opposition in the Ontario legislature insisted that there should be no anti-British sentiments expressed in universities. Canada was a British colony and therefore had no room for anti-British expressions. More significantly, he went on to say that this issue was not one of freedom of speech but rather an issue of the basic conception of the role of the university in a British society. He said that just as a priest who went outside a church and ridiculed religion would clearly have no place as a priest in the institution of the church, a professor who promoted decolonization and Canadian sovereignty should not teach in an Ontario university.[1]

Again and again, under the pressures of changing social values, professors and administrators inside the university redefine the boundaries of acceptable behaviour. Put differently, even though you can only be fired from a university for "cause," moral turpitude has always been the primary cause for which you can be fired, and moral turpitude gets redefined in each generation and in each moral crisis of the culture.

During McCarthyism in the United States, the same problem arose. Universities needed to eject people who were considered unpatriotic without seeming to jeopardize academic freedom, so they worked out a way to get rid of all the people who took the Fifth Amendment. When some investigating committees demanded to know whether certain professors were Communists, and when these individuals failed to disclose whether they were Communists, such faculty members were said to lack candour. Clearly, it was argued, if you are going to be in a university, you owe an obligation to your colleagues to disclose your political affiliations. If you are not going to be candid and if you are not going to answer to the inquisition, then you are by definition unfit to be a professor. Suddenly, "lack of candour" became the new form of moral turpitude.[2]

We are witnessing a similar kind of accommodation. With the collaboration of professors and also, unfortunately, with assistance from sections even of the Canadian Association of University Teachers, which fought so heroically in the past for the institution of academic freedom, the corporate community of the universities is once again seeking to redefine the boundaries of acceptable behaviour by excluding from the protections of academic freedom certain moral and cultural positions having to do with a broad range of gender and race issues often misleadingly defined under the banner of human rights "abuses."

I want to repeat my contention that academic freedom is not nearly strong enough. Some say that academics have too much power. But, as I documented in *Moral Panic,* power in the university is most obviously deployed when the employer turns against an employee. Power is used and abused when Professor Matin Yaqzan is eased out of his employment at the University of New Brunswick because he expresses unpopular opinions about a controversial issue of sexual politics. Power is visibly used and misused when Professor Warren Magnusson at the University of Victoria is dragged through sexual harassment procedures for two years as a result of writing an article calling feminist fundamentalism into question. Power is both unmistakable and in service of opaque ulterior motives when Professor Lucinda Vandervort, a feminist lawyer at the University of Saskatchewan, is nearly fired for reasons of "insensitivity" when she purportedly allows a student to come out as a lesbian to a small seminar. University officials knew that the young woman in question was in fact campaigning openly for a position in student politics as a lesbian, but they nevertheless used this incident to deny the protection of academic freedom to the teacher and put her employment in jeopardy. Similarly, in Ontario, Professor Heinz Klatt at King's

College, Professor Marjorie Ratcliffe at the University of Western Ontario, Professor Paul Lamy at the University of Ottawa, and Professor Ken Westhues at the University of Waterloo have all suffered through extensive and damaging proceedings for allegedly committing ill-defined speech crimes in violation of newly emerging norms of decorum in Canadian universities. In these cases, and others like them from coast to coast, *civility* is the control code in the name of which intrusive power is unjustifiably exercised.[3]

Another Canadian story of this kind is the extraordinary case of a professor at Queen's University who early in 1994 took a class of graduate students on a field trip to a Caribbean island. When he got back to his university, he was formally accused of "insensitivity to female students," particularly their diets, not least because he had supplied his students with spicy local Caribbean food as well as French brie and croissants. After two years of laborious university process and questionable treatment by his department, a decanal investigative committee, and a grievance panel, he had still to attend what they call the ultimate tribunal, the final stage in Queen's internal procedure (unless he were to start with something entirely different because the procedures had meanwhile changed). Only after all such internal steps were exhausted would the disposition of this case be subject to judicial review. As of mid-1997, this farcical institutional harassment of a long-term, award-winning employee had already cost the professor his health, his salary, and $40,000 in lawyer's fees.

It is not only this Canadian scientist in particular that we need to have regard for – and I am certainly not relaying this story as a typical examplmuch I know that I ought to make us how slight of the few that and misguided personal harassment exists in the world. My point is that very significant abuses can arise out of careless processes and unexamined or misdirected social agendas. One of our responsibilities as intellectuals is to speak back not only to power but also to "progressive" movements that cause abuses. If we do not, we repeat the history of the many kinds of petty totalitarian distortions with which Utopian thought has gifted us in the twentieth century.

We must expand the project of academic freedom. It is not a completed project. It has won us the right to do the work we need to do in the classroom; it has won us the right to keep our civil and political rights without losing our jobs. We must not retreat from that. We must continue to expand academic freedom so that not only academics currently working in the universities have the broad cultural freedoms required to do their jobs but also all the new people arriving in the universities acquire the right to do their work freely. The undesirable alternative, however forcefully it may be propped up by moralistic posturing, is the construction of a legacy of orthodoxy, a legacy of the persecution of heretics. This latter alternative downgrades not only the academics who promote or accommodate it but also the value of higher education and the university itself.

To give strategic meaning and relevance to the concept of academic freedom, we must find a definition that brings to the foreground the right to
offend. I do not mean that we should aim to be uncivil. I do not mean that
we should brutalize our students. I do not mean that Canadian professors
have a licence to behave in ways that are totally un-Canadian. I do not have
in mind that we promote these commonsensical ethical violations. Indeed,
these problems are red herrings. The problem we are facing is not one of
rude professors getting ruder and out of control.

The problem we are facing is that a program of *taking offence* is wreaking
havoc in the university. So, if we are going to define and preserve academic
freedom at this time and leave a legacy for tomorrow, then we have to insist
that we will not surrender to those who are taking offence. In the absence
of a credible cultural authority – and what we have in our times is not a
credible cultural authority but a great division of many voices in many debates – no society can usefully legislate culture: neither "appropriate" language nor "appropriate" gender relations. In our society, there is neither
authority nor warrant for a *command* culture.

If, as do advocates of "inclusiveness," we say that race and gender are the
most important features of social life and personal identity, how can we
then be forbidden to talk about them? Or how can we talk about them
only in ways that are authorized by some interests and not by others? How
can we, especially in the university, close down the widest possible discussion of these issues and reduce the chances that, through discussion and
debate, the aspects of them that we care about can sift out and prevail, or
that the aspects of them that we find distressing can be deplored and perhaps remedied? In short, how can we agree to preempt the ongoing cultural
debates in the formation of culture and submit instead to patently premia-
ture, quasi-judicial determination and mure-particular administration of cultural development?

People take offence in universities in two institutional ways, and both
ways are increasingly familiar. The first is the *individual* taking of offence,
when suffered or perceived slights are translated into some kind of juridical
process. This way amounts to submitting the force, the conflict, and sometimes the pain of ideas to the emotional tyranny of individual vulnerabili-
ties. The second is the *political* taking of offence, which, in the critical legal
movement in the United States, has already resulted in the explicit suggestion that corrective stratification of speech rights ought to occur: people
defined by some authority as disadvantaged should have more speech
rights, and people defined by some authority as not disadvantaged should
have fewer speech rights. Expansion of speaking opportunity for some
would give way to zero tolerance of inappropriate speech for others. The
imperfections of liberal society, ever ready for self-reforming improvement,
would be subsumed under an officially sanctioned Hobbesian solution in

the illiberal state. Of course, if we imagine the kind of bureaucracy needed to implement and manage such an official system of differential entitlements to inquiry and expression, and if we consider the kinds of police involvement, the kinds of adjudication, the kinds of assessment and enforcement required to organize and keep dynamic such a system of inequality in the name of equity, we may justly conclude that this regression to Leviathan is a dystopian nightmare for society and not the way to go. As for the university and its special, long-term intellectual mission on behalf of civilization, such dystopia is literally a dead end.

We have to remember that the intrusive university is the university of censorship, both prohibitive and hortatory. One can argue against this kind of censorship from the vantage point of antifoundationalism, on the grounds that we do not know as much as we think we know. And one can argue against it from the viewpoint of professionalism, on the grounds that we do know some things, and we want to have our arguments in the classrooms and not the courtrooms. We can also say no to official censorship in the universities because we want to let universities be self-reforming institutions. The bottom line is that restricting freedom of expression by regulative or legal measures for high moral reasons or high civic reasons, whatever they may be, always leads to a constant stream of continuing abuses. We would be very unwise to collaborate in this restriction to the academy and to ourselves.

### Notes

1 Michiel Horn, "The Mildew of Discretion: Academic Freedom and Self-Censorship," *Dalhousie Review* 72.4 (1992-3): 439-66. See especially page 453 for George Drew's reasons for urging that University of Toronto professor Frank Underhill be disciplined for advocating Canadian sovereignty in an essay. York University historian Horn's writing is the most extensive scholarship now available on censorship, self-censorship, and related issues of discipline in Canadian universities before the current stage of harassment panic and "political correctness." He shows the extent to which freedom of speech is regularly ranked below other loyalties. See Michiel Horn, *Academic Freedom in Canada: A History* (Toronto: University of Toronto Press, 1999).

2 Ellen Schrecker, "Academic Freedom: The Historical View," in *Regulating the Intellectuals: Perspectives on Academic Freedom in the 1980s*, eds. Craig Kaplan and Ellen Schrecker (New York: Praeger, 1983), 38. Schrecker's work is particularly useful for documenting harassment of the Left, but her study of McCarthyism shows more clearly than other texts the general mechanisms of conformist peer accommodation and defence of the academy at the expense of the professional freedoms of dissenting individual academics. It provides a cautionary lesson for a time when the same wind is blowing the other way.

3 John Fekete, *Moral Panic: Biopolitics Rising* (Montreal and Toronto: Robert Davies, 1994). *Moral Panic* is the first book to document extensively the fallout of the harassment panic in Canadian universities and to provide detailed accounts of the accusations and proceedings against seventeen professors from 1988 to 1994. The context is a study of the self-feeding sex-and-violence panic of the late 1980s and early 1990s in Canada, and an analysis of the sexual politics of that panic which, underpinned by distorted statistics, presented a false if influential image of society as engaged in a relentless war against women.

# 10
# The New Sectarianism and the Liberal University
*Graham Good*

University life in Canada is increasingly affected by the new sectarianism: the categorization of people by race, gender, and sexual preference. Both the individuality of humans and their membership in the universal category of humanity are rejected or downplayed in favour of specific categories of identity. These categories are felt to divide human experience so radically that a person from one category should not or cannot speak about the experience of a person from another category. They are the modern equivalents of the "estates" of prerevolutionary France or the "classes" of traditional Marxism. Each individual belongs to at least three categories: white or nonwhite, male or female, heterosexual or homosexual. The first category in each case is perceived as dominant, the second as oppressed.

The new sectarianism (or "categoryism") can be defined as understanding human experience primarily in terms of the identity-category of the experiencer and as reversing the previous power relations to prefer the second within each pair of categories. Thus, if you are a heterosexual, white male, categoryism awards you three minuses. The phrase "white male" is reminiscent of a police description or a zoological classification, and new sectarian discourse is almost always the prelude to abuse and denigration.

The new sectarianism does not create equality but merely reverses previous inequalities of respect. It perpetuates an atmosphere where certain kinds of people are preferred to certain others – all that changes are the preferences. To see a person primarily as a "white male" or a "gay female" is to diminish their humanity and their individuality. It suggests that their experience is contained within the group category and is fundamentally (not just partially) distinct from the experience of those in other categories. It also minimizes the differences among individuals within the category.

Structures of preference among the categories of a population inevitably create resentment in those who are not preferred; they in turn put forward their claim to be oppressed and to have the order of preference changed once again. Males are beginning to think of themselves as the newest victim group, denigrated in the media, discriminated against in family law, more liable to imprisonment, suicide, and early death, and condemned to the dirtiest and least safe work. The only long-term solution to discrimination is a system of strict nonpreference between categories; that is, treating people primarily as individuals irrespective of categories.

Most societies have been based on a hierarchy of class, ethnicity, and gender; where they have differed is the order of preference. Only the liberal humanist vision (approached but never achieved) aims to do away with the ladder rather than change its order of priority. The Marxist vision has classlessness as its eventual goal but only after a temporary intensification of class struggle known as "the dictatorship of the proletariat." The new sectarianism rarely provides a clear vision of the future it desires, because it cannot contemplate the weakening or virtual disappearance of categorization that full equality would entail.

Yet the new sectarianism uses the liberal rhetoric of justice and fairness when it is strategically convenient. Contemporary activism tends to start with equality claims appealing to the liberal conscience but then to move on to an explicit or implicit claim of superiority. This claim can sound like the original prejudice in reverse. For example, in the 1950s and earlier, women were considered unsuited to university education because they were less intellectual than emotional. Feminism rightly denied this stereotype in a claim for equal access to higher education, only to reassert it in the claim that women are essentially more cooperative, more supportive, more related, less competitive, less hierarchical, and so on and that institutions should be "feminized" to reflect the superiority of feminine values. In fact, what universities need is to be humanized rather than further divided by gender and other categories.

Although group organization has played a major role in overcoming prejudice, the change in public opinion over the last thirty to forty years has occurred largely through arguments based on liberal ideas of fairness to individuals, regardless (as it used to be said) of "class, creed, or colour." People have come to respect the claim for equal treatment and perhaps for that reason to resist claims for preferential treatment. Past disadvantage should be remedied by present equality, not by special new advantages. Categoryism should be dissolved rather than preserved in a new form. Treating people as individuals rather than category members is just as antiracist, antisexist, and antihomophobic as the group approach and, in the long run, it is probably the best guarantee of security against discrimination. But unfortunately, individualism is out of favour with intellectuals who are enamoured of new versions of the collectivist ideologies of the thirties and forties.

The new sectarianism poses a serious threat to the humanist principle in teaching. If students are not treated primarily as individuals but as "representatives" of their demographic category, their dignity and autonomy are diminished. Often, false assumptions are made about individuals on the basis of their group. For example, advocates of the "sensitive" approach to teaching might assert that Asian females are reluctant to participate in class discussion because of cultural conditioning that has to be overcome by special strategies. In effect, this view is prejudicial, even if it is intended to be helpful. The group is still stereotyped. In my twenty-five years of teaching classes with high proportions of Asian students, I have found there is no correlation between race and gender on the one hand and volubility and taciturnity on the other.

In the "categorized" classroom, students are taken as representatives, speaking for and from their group. This arrangement discourages them from expressing views contrary to what the "sensitive" teacher expects of them. A "progressive" teacher who believes "We live in a racist society" can exert a strong control over opinions expressed in class. Members of minorities may be reluctant to say that they are not discriminated against to any significant degree. Ironically, to state this view may actually create discrimination against them in the classroom because they have said the wrong thing. They may be told directly or indirectly that they are deceiving themselves, are suffering from false consciousness, or are in denial. When views are ascribed or even prescribed to students according to their race and gender, they may be shamed as not truly belonging to their category if they hold different opinions. The emphasis on "diversity" of demographic category can end up by repressing a genuine diversity of individual opinion.

Already becoming common, though not yet mandatory, are workshops in "unlearning sexism" or "unlearning racism." Here, the starting assumption is that participants are harbouring prejudices, even if those prejudices are unconscious. The goal is to bring about a confession of guilt and then reward the penitent with forgiveness. These workshops are reminiscent of the confessional totalitarianism examined in Orwell's *1984,* the self-criticism sessions under Communism, or inquisitions into heresy and devil worship under theocracies.

In some "diversity" workshops, the new sectarian view of human behaviour is enforced by physically grouping participants according to various distinctions: male and female, Jew and Gentile, gay and straight, and so forth. Everyone says how they "feel" about these divisions as they look across at the other group. These exercises run the risk of reinforcing the very divisions they are intended to overcome. The presupposition is that those divisions are very deep and must be demonstrated and acknowledged before they can be healed. Confession has to precede atonement. Ruled out is the possibility (which for most people is a daily lived reality) that friendly understanding, civility, and respect are normal in interactions with others, whether or not they belong to a different race or gender. The feeling-controllers have to first inculpate you so that they can then exonerate you and leave you confessed and shriven.

The university should be dedicated to reason, not feeling. It may study emotion, but it should not encourage displays of emotion. Yet the university is increasingly seen by "equity" advocates as a community of feeling, not as a community of reason. The new sectarianism is much concerned about how people "feel" in the classroom and elsewhere, and somewhat less concerned about how they think. Indeed, in extreme cases, clarity and logic are disparaged as patriarchal values.

Universities are beginning routinely to attribute to their members feelings based on race and gender categories. White males are assumed to harbour in some degree feelings of racism and sexism. Women are assumed to feel victimized and in constant danger of insult, aggression, and assault. Minorities are assumed to suffer regular slights, discrimination, and hostility. These strategies undermine basic principles of justice. Everyone has individual responsibility for his or her own words and actions, and not for those of others in his or her demographic group. Everyone has the right to be considered innocent until proven guilty. These principles are being ignored as Canadian universities move toward holding white males collectively guilty of imputed feelings of racism and sexism. These feelings are held to be as inescapable and all-pervasive as "sin" in some theocratic societies or "counterrevolutionary tendencies" in some Communist dictatorships. Will the next step be inquisitions, confessions, and atonements under the guise of workshops, counselling, and sensitivity training?

The university has to insist on civility and respect in its members' behaviour toward each other, but it should not enter the terrain of their private feelings. Nor should it impose its own official "constructions" of these feelings onto its members by demographic category. There should be a positive right to be treated by the university as individuals, not as representatives of categories. The only categories the university can legitimately create are "student," "instructor," or "department head," which denote positions within the academic structure. It has no right to make presumptions of the type that Asian females need special help to participate in class discussions.

These kinds of categorization can be offensive and anti-individualist, yet it is hard to convince people who have accepted the new sectarian view. They have grown accustomed to judging people according to category and "constructing" individuals as group members, often determining their attitude toward what you say by which group you belong to. Thus, if an argument emanates from a white male, the new sectarian will expect, or at least suspect, that it is a pretext for protecting patriarchal privilege. There's little point in paying close attention or in trying to refute the argument. Rather than judge the argument on its merits, the sectarian judges it on the basis of who is speaking. Conversely, even highly dubious arguments may go unchallenged if their proponents belong to "oppressed" categories. Both the suspicion and the indulgence are disrespectful. Equality of respect demands that you give the same attention to each speaker and agree or disagree according to your view about the argument, not according to the demographic category of the speaker.

A new politics of feeling is emerging on campus, using nebulous metaphors like "chilly climate" and "hostile environment" for any incident that doesn't "feel right" or "feels uncomfortable." "Systemic discrimination" is another vague concept, where discrimination is constructed not as conscious and individual but as unconscious and collective. Normal, well-meaning people are held to be unwittingly acting in ways that "exclude" certain demographic groups. To overcome this problem, they are told they need to be "sensitized," their feelings and behaviour modified to what equity officials see as desirable. The university becomes a school of manners, teaching "appropriate" facial and verbal expressions. Or it becomes a theatre of symbolic redress, where penitents atone for the past sins of their category.

In this new economy of feeling, emotions are treated as collective, not individual. Feeling has a place in the literary aspect of liberal education, and this aspect constitutes a partial exception to the sovereignty of reason. But here distinctiveness of personal response is the focus, not the politics of group responses. Emotions are individual – those expressed by the poet, implicit in the poem, or evoked in the reader. This view has been replaced by such collective concepts as "interpretive communities" that determine the limits of acceptable interpretation. "I feel" is replaced by "We feel," "I think" by "We think." The university becomes an affirmative "community," representing and "celebrating" the diversity of the groups (except white males) that comprise it, but not the diversity of individuals.

The university is changing from a place where professors teach students how to think, into a place where officials teach professors what to feel. These bureaucrats claim special expertise in "equity issues" not possessed by other members of the university. Their "skills" are needed, they claim, because professors are not adept at "human management" and need experts to make judgments for them. When my department was warned that studying literature does not equip us to give advice or make judgments on matters of discrimination and harassment, the whole traditional justification for studying the humanities was casually discarded. The idea of human relations as a special professional skill is a denial of the very basis of the "humanities": forming a well-rounded personality capable of ethical judgment as *a human,* not as an expert.

This humane individualism only gradually came to include all categories of humanity. Excluded groups were amply justified in claiming access
to this liberal ideal of freedom and respect. Initially, the demand for inclusion was framed in liberal terms: the newcomers, having been excluded as
groups, sought inclusion in the university and other institutions as individuals. Only later did some seek to reconstitute the groups, claiming that
continuing disadvantage within the institution justified special group privileges and advantages known as "educational equity." Yet many individuals do not wish to be identified with these "equity-seeking groups," nor do
they wish the group spokespersons to speak for them. Yet publicly dissoci-
ating themselves from the group's ideological positions could carry heavy
penalties, which not all are willing to pay. Thus, the impression of group
unity triumphs.

Progress in the last fifty years toward equality of respect and away from
various forms of prejudice has largely been achieved through the appeal to
liberal humanist principles. Yet after that process was well under way, it was
captured by those who denied that significant progress had been made and
who asserted that the small improvement was threatened by an imminent
"backlash." Though Freudo-Marxist radicals often accuse others of being
"in denial," it never occurs to them to wonder if they are "in denial" of the
actual tolerance everywhere in evidence around them. Thus a Soviet-style
gap opens between an ideology of continuing struggle against "oppression"
and the reality of rapidly diminishing prejudice and growing tolerance. Men,
having for the most part helped or at least acquiesced in the progress of
women into formerly masculine preserves, are subjected by some feminists
to ever more ferocious denunciations and cries of "backlash," while remain-
ing pockets of resistance are magnified out of all proportion. Despite the
manifestly greater openness to minorities in society, whites are told that
they are still crypto-racist or that the "system" is still racist, even if no one
consciously intends it to be so. The widespread legal and social acceptance
of homosexuality is not usually met with celebration of this increased tolerance but more often with intensifying accusations of "homophobia."
The accusers take advantage of the liberal climate to call it "chilly" for
themselves.

In the university, the new sectarianism leads to a concept of cultural property: each sect claims exclusive rights to teach works by or about their sect,
except that the work of white males can be taught by anyone. Thus, a white
male instructor who offers a course in literature by women of colour is likely
to be accused of "appropriation of voice," though if he omits them from a
more general course, he will be accused of "marginalizing" or "silencing"
the voices of the oppressed. Yet no one suggests that white males have a
special understanding of Shakespeare or that only they should be allowed
to teach his work. The application of the new sectarianism is asymmetrical

in this regard. The rule of cultural property propounds that the teacher should belong to the same race, gender, and sexual orientation, even ethnic background, as the works being taught, except in the case of white males. The rule also seems to suggest that students will profit most from studies of their own sect, fortifying them in their sectarian identity rather than widening and challenging it. The humanist dictum "Nothing human is alien to me" becomes "Everything human is alien to me except my own race-gender-sexual orientation."

Gender studies is perhaps the most prominent example of the new sectarianism, having greater numbers and influence than gay and lesbian studies or race-based studies. Gender studies is virtually a female preserve in the university, and feminist researchers work to define the roles and identities not only of women but also of men. Male "constructions" of women are deconstructed but not women's of men. Men's depictions of women are assumed to be false, especially if they have negative elements in them. They need correction, whereas women's images of men are assumed to be accurate.

The only substantial work on men's identity from a nonfeminist viewpoint has been done outside the university by men's movement writers and workshop leaders such as Robert Bly, Michael Meade, and Sam Keene. Their work has had little academic impact because university men rarely attend their activities or read their books. The general attitude among academic men is an embarrassed acceptance of the press caricature of the movement as consisting of drumming and running naked in the woods – a level of understanding equivalent to seeing the women's movement as a bunch of bra burners.

Why have male academics given feminists a monopoly on gender studies? There are several possible reasons. Feminists created the subject and retain a proprietary attitude toward it, so men feel like trespassers. Occasionally, a profeminist male might propose research or teaching about gender from a feminist viewpoint, but this situation is rare. Some men might feel that self-consciousness about gender roles is somehow unmanly and best left to women. Or it might seem that working on gender would lead to subservience to feminism, or to conflict, neither being attractive prospects. The avoidance of conflict may be a result of residual "chivalry" or to early conditioning that fighting girls is much worse than fighting boys. Or liberal men may feel "gender guilt" and believe that it's women's turn to be "heard" after the lengthy male dominance of the university.

The usual solution of male academics to the problem of gender studies is to keep silent or to make deferential gestures toward feminism and then turn away to focus their research on general or "nongendered" issues. In other words, the gendered perspective of feminism is not matched by a gendered masculine perspective but by a humanist one. Now, some would immediately claim that this nongendered humanist perspective is a sham:

it is actually men's studies. But this claim neglects the great difference between men-as-representative-humans and men-as-males. Traditional humanism talked about "Man" and "men", not "males." Women were implicitly included in "Man" as a species term, even though the assumptions about this creature admittedly fitted the male better than the female. But this fact does not make nongendered humanist studies into men's studies. An odd asymmetry results: men are seen by feminists as occupying "gendered subject positions" but by themselves as having a general, humanist outlook.

How will this situation develop? There are several possibilities. One is that the female will replace the male as the representative human being, the norm of the species against which the other gender is seen as a special case: an abnormal, defective, or lesser human. In this scenario, woman will become man, while men will become the second sex. This change would be equivalent to the Marxist goal of the proletariat replacing the bourgeoisie as the universal class, the provider of human norms for other classes to imitate.

Another possibility is that humanist studies will decline and perish, leaving all the humanities as gender studies. The known world will be divided into men's studies and women's studies. The problem here would be the vast amount of indispensable knowledge left to the men's side. To have this enormous achievement being taught by men to men as a celebration of specifically masculine rather than human creativity would be unacceptable to most feminists. They would want to retain ideological control of this material to ensure that any positive aspects of this heritage were counterbalanced or cancelled by a stress on its oppressive, patriarchal, and imperialistic character and by magnifying and celebrating an oppositional female achievement. "Difference" is not pushed far enough to make traditional humanist culture an exclusively masculine concern that feminists should completely reject. The logic of "difference," if carried to its conclusion, would lead back to separate, single-sex institutions of higher education, but no one is currently advocating this solution.

Thus the gendering of the university curriculum is likely to remain incomplete. The approaches will probably continue to be an uneasy combination of gendered and ungendered, feminist and humanist, with most men and some women centred on humanism with marginal gestures toward feminism, and some women centred on feminism with appropriations of humanist perspectives when needed. An eventual possibility, however, is that all subjects would be taught by all teachers from a feminist viewpoint: feminism will essentially absorb or become humanism.

The irony is that gender difference is asserted more and more strongly as it lessens in practice. Men's and women's lives are actually becoming more and more alike, involving similar responsibilities in the workplace and at home. The contradiction between difference claims and parity (or gender balance) claims becomes evident if we juxtapose them: "Men and women are very different and should therefore do all the same jobs." (This contradiction is usually kept hidden by keeping the two parts of the statement separate.) Why should we strive to have more male nurses and female engineers if the two genders have radically different cultures and ways of knowing and interrelating, which would naturally lead them to different interests and occupations? The demand for gender balance is in any case selective in practice. The focus is on equal representation in powerful, desirable, middle-class jobs, not in dirty, dangerous, working-class jobs like construction, mining, and logging – still largely masculine preserves.

Difference and sameness arguments are in fact normally applied selectively, depending on which will get the best result for women. In positive contexts, parity is emphasized: women are equally capable of climbing mountains, climbing corporate ladders, or playing sports like boxing, rugby, and so on. But if the context is negative, the same activities can be stereotyped as masculine, hierarchical, and competitive, and thus women, with their nurturing, collaborative natures, are seen as morally superior to them. Equality for women is not claimed in negative activities. Many believe in a female divinity, few in a female devil. Often people pause when they use the phrase "the white man" when talking about imperialism, wondering for a moment if they should substitute a gender-neutral alternative. But no, the context is negative, thus a male, noninclusive term is still appropriate.

The contradictions and double standards are also evident in the charged area of violence. Male violence is seen as typical, female violence exceptional. If a woman is violent toward a man, she is assumed to have been provoked beyond endurance by male oppression. But the idea that male violence toward a woman may have been provoked by the woman's behaviour is treated as odious, repugnant, blame-the-victim thinking. Thus male violence is due to male aggressivity, and so is female violence. The "battered wife syndrome" is being used to reduce the jail sentences of women who kill their husbands, but there is no equivalent "provoked husband" syndrome to reduce male culpability.

There is a similar contradiction over images of women. Some feminists extol the virtues of ancient goddess cults, even though the emphasis on fertility is often reflected in figures with grossly exaggerated breasts and buttocks. But when other images emphasize the same features of the female body, they are considered to objectify women for the delectation of the male gaze. In addition, goddess feminists neglect the fact that the modern women's movement owes its existence in large part to the control of fertility through contraception and abortion, which is precisely the opposite of the values represented by the goddess.

Another false assumption of the new sectarianism is that white males have been dominant throughout history by virtue of their race and gender.

This assumption completely ignores the fact that the vast majority of white males have been subjected to oppression and exploitation as much as any other group. It would have been small comfort to them to know that their oppressors were frequently other white males. The new sectarianism seems oblivious to the capacity of members of any group to inflict suffering on members of their own group. Exploitation does not require difference: some of the worst suffering in history has been imposed by people who belonged to the same demographic category as their victims.

What does the future look like under the new sectarianism? We could see the university become a cultural battleground for competing identity-categories based on race, gender, and sexuality, which could themselves further divide into proliferating subcategories. We could see attempts at strictly proportional representation, where the university tries to reproduce at every level the demographic composition of the general population, despite the difficulty of establishing reliable statistics on changeable identity factors like sexual preference. These attempts at demographic control could further centralize power in university administrations and diminish the autonomy of departments. All of these trends should be countered by a new emphasis on treating members of the university as individuals, not as representatives of groups.

The new sectarian emphasis on feeling must be countered by a stronger emphasis on intellectual quest. Emotional comfort cannot be a valid goal for university education, which should challenge rather than reinforce existing assumptions and identities. Knowledge should not be preselected and filtered to support an existing world view. We need to reassert the liberal-humanist principle that the study of experiences, perspectives, and cultures remote from one's own is immensely valuable. Students should be told, "Knowledge should change you. You should not demand that knowledge change to suit you by conforming to your current predilections. Learning means learning that reality is often not as you suppose it to be. It means coping with the emotional discomfort of qualifying ardently held views, acknowledging irony and complexity, and even admitting you are wrong."

To be true to the ideals of the liberal university, we need to give clear priority to the individual intellect over the group-based emotionalism fostered by the new sectarianism. We need to reemphasize what we all share as human individuals, to prevent the acknowledgment of group difference from intensifying into the politics of group division.

# 11
# Judaic Studies and Western Civilization: Identity Politics and the Academy
*Harvey Shulman*

In July 1996, after holding office for only two weeks, Professor Thomas Bird resigned as director of the Queens College Judaic studies program. His withdrawal followed public controversy over his qualifications and religion. Bird, a Catholic and since 1965 a professor of Yiddish at Queens College, was an activist on behalf of numerous Jewish causes, among them a trip to the USSR on behalf of Soviet Jewry. His letter of resignation noted that "it is impossible not to conclude that the attempt to trash my academic record and standing in the Jewish community through insinuation and omission is anything other than a fig leaf for objections to my being a Gentile" and that he was "the object of primitive religious bigotry."

In late October 1996, Bird and two Jewish colleagues were named interim directors of the program while a search for a permanent director took place. As of 1 April 1997, no appointment had been announced for a program registering 500 to 800 students in a number of interdisciplinary courses primarily taught by faculty borrowed from appropriate departments; Judaic studies had no permanent staff.

Controversy surrounding Bird's resignation was widespread. All three New York City dailies ran articles. Further notice appeared in the American and the Israeli press as well as in the *Washington Post, New Republic,* and *Chronicle of Higher Education.* The dispute constituted one more illustration of disagreement between the life of the mind and the life of ethnic engagement. As with black and women's studies programs, Jewish studies also experienced tension and division over its raison d'être, its intellectual merit, and its curriculum design.

Professor Samuel Heilman, a colleague of Bird's and a previous head of the Judaic studies program, led the opposition to Bird's appointment on grounds that he was not qualified to assume the office because he lacked scholarly credentials, Hebrew competence, and a completed doctorate. It seems that Bird's thesis defence at Princeton was unduly delayed because two of his dissertation advisors had died. In a letter to the Jewish *Forward,*

Heilman further elaborated his reasons for opposing Bird's appointment. He acknowledged Bird's competence to teach Yiddish, but he argued that the program director needed to act as a role model for the students and community, and he defended the symbolic importance of appointing Jews to head the program: "That is why at Queens College the head of the black and African studies program is from Ethiopia, the head of Irish studies is of Irish descent, and the head of Italian studies, Italian American."[1] For Heilman, the director "is more than just a teacher. He's someone who stands for the group."[2] Rabbi Joseph Sungolowsky, a professor of Judaic studies and French literature, and Bird's predecessor as director, also argued that a Jewish academic must head the program, because a non-Jew "cannot be culturally and emotionally in tune with the students and with the members of the Jewish community."[3]

Many of Bird's other detractors focused solely on what they believed to be his inadequate academic credentials to head a Jewish studies program. Professor Lawrence Schiffman, a distinguished New York University scholar of rabbinic Judaism and the Dead Sea scrolls, as well as program director of the Association of Jewish Studies, criticized Queens College for substituting parochial Jewish community interests for the academic needs of its program: "The cat is finally out of the bag ... There are two kinds of Jewish studies in this country: serious academic study of the historical experience of the Jews in all its historical, literary and cultural manifestations done at a small number of universities, and a much more widespread form of Jewish ethnic studies."[4] Richard Siegel, executive director of the National Foundation for Jewish Culture, argued that Jewish studies is not about group affirmation but about the study of texts and ideas with Hebrew a basic requirement.[5]

Rabbi Allan Nadler, with a PhD from Harvard and director of research at YIVO[6] Institute for Jewish Research, wrote that Bird's religion was irrelevant but that he lacked the necessary credentials to head the program. Nadler enumerated the scholarly and disciplinary requirements of a respected, academically sound program, including mastery in Hebrew, Aramaic, and Syriac as well as Yiddish, Ladino, and Judeo-Arabic. He also argued that Judaic studies must not become another ethnic studies program of dubious intellectual merit.[7] The insistence on linguistic competence as a necessary requirement for Jewish studies preceded the Queens College dispute. In a 1993 article in *Judaism,* Professor Bernard Cooperman of Brooklyn College argued, "Literacy implies intimate knowledge of Hebrew and at least reading knowledge of Yiddish, Aramaic and three or four other languages that Jews and Jewish scholarship have used over the centuries. The crucial test which defines whether someone is a legitimate member of the profession or a mere 'interloper' in Jewish Studies is whether or not that person has a working knowledge of Hebrew."[8]

Martin Jaffee, professor of Jewish studies at the University of Washington, notes that the head of that program, a student of medieval Jewish thought, was also not Jewish: "The fact that he is not a role model of Jewish commitment never occurred to us. In our view, the most effective role model in Jewish studies is supplied by those who believe that the study of Jews and Judaism demands the most serious intellectual preparation and rewards the prepared scholar with deep insights into the human condition."[9] It is noteworthy that both Bird's protagonists and supporters claimed the imprimatur of opposition to ethnocentrism and some of the anti-intellectual qualities attributed to black and women's studies. Many of Bird's faculty supporters were displeased with the nonacademic issues surrounding the controversy and were intent on separating themselves from any hint of ghettoized ethnocentrism.

Queens College president Allen Sessoms defended the Bird appointment, noting "it is shameful that a scholar of Professor Bird's reputation should be subjected to a campaign of intolerance."[10] In response to the accusation of failing to consult before making the appointment, Sessoms stated that he vetted Bird's name with selected Jewish organizations and with Nobel Prize recipient Elie Wiesel. Sessoms called Heilman's attempts to undermine the Bird appointment "academic guerrilla warfare at its worst."[11] Ammiel Alcaly, chair of the department that houses the Hebrew and Yiddish programs, criticized Heilman's parochialism and praised Bird's "energy and erudition as a humanist."[12]

The argument that competence in Hebrew is a basic requirement for a director of a Jewish studies program was disputed. Johnathan Helfand, professor of modern Jewish history at Brooklyn College, stated that Hebrew is not required in all areas of Jewish studies.[13] Professor Robert Seltzer, head of the Association for Jewish Studies, stated that neither lacking Hebrew nor being a non-Jew should disqualify anyone from assuming the Queens College position of director of Judaic studies.[14]

Former dean and professor emeritus Ernest Schwarcz wrote to the *Forward* to praise Bird's academic credentials and years of service on behalf of Jewish causes. He also raised the issue of Jewish and white teachers in the city and remarked on the Jewish community's traditional rejection of ethnic or colour tests for educators. Schwarcz noted, "When we established the program some 26 years ago, we were guided by the philosophy that Judaism, Jewish values and ethics are among the mainstays of Western civilization and should be presented as such."[15] A tenured professor at a Catholic university, Professor Bernard Stern, also a contributor to the *Forward,* wrote: "Tell me, is Professor Sungolowsky [an opponent of Bird's appointment and the previous director], professor of French Literature, a Frenchman? Shame on you, Queens College provincials!"[16]

Scholars across the United States entered the controversy. Professor Eugene Genovese, a prominent historian of the Civil War and slavery, said that to demand Bird's resignation "is to say that the purpose of the college is not intellectual work but ideological indoctrination."[17] Robert R. Sullivan, professor of criminal justice at John Jay College, wrote that Bird's resignation "shows what's wrong with racial, ethnic, religious and gender programs in colleges and universities: They are not committed to objective study designed to produce reliable knowledge. Rather, their primary commitments are political, social or psychological. The Queens College affair provides the best of arguments for ending such programs."[18]

Rabbi Arthur Hertzberg, a distinguished professor of French Enlightenment history, stated that the major problem is not whether a non-Jew should head a Jewish studies program but if "Jewish studies belong together with black studies, Hispanic studies, feminist studies and the like, or whether learning and research in Judaica belongs to the mainstream of academic concerns."[19] Accordingly, he dismissed claims of Bird's scholarly unsuitability to head the Judaic studies program at Queens. For Hertzberg, it was unreasonable to expect the director of any program to be familiar with the range of specialized areas and disciplines, major texts, and historical watersheds of the field. As well, the *Washington Post* saw Bird's appointment and subsequent resignation as illustrative of larger ethical and intellectual problems afflicting universities. The *Post* asked if "so-called ethnic studies programs, whether Afro-American, Hispanic or Asian American or Jewish, are to be arenas for open inquiry. Or are they to be a kind of intellectual spoils system, with each teaching its own youth its own version of life, culture and history?"[20]

Although the rhetoric of inclusivity and diversity accompanies ethnic study programs, they often exclude and isolate faculty who express divergent viewpoints. Some of the best women academics very quickly leave women's studies programs or refuse to participate in them because of the extra-academic agenda and antidisciplinary pursuits of their participants. At Emory University, Professor Elizabeth Fox-Genovese experienced unusual difficulties when she tried to build an intellectually respectable women's studies program, free of feminist ideology. While conducting interviews for a book on women's studies programs, Professors Daphne Patai and Noretta Koertge had to assure reluctant faculty that their opinions would remain anonymous. They attribute this reluctance to "the tendency of feminism to stifle open debate and create an atmosphere in which disagreement is viewed as betrayal."[21] Far fewer in numbers than women professors, African-American scholars often feel compelled to participate in black studies initiatives, even at the expense of their disciplinary research. For some, the ideological underpinnings of these "studies" programs become intolerant and untenable, and they leave.[22]

Attempts by faculty and administration to transform the university have elicited critical reactions from academics. Sandford Pinsker, a Franklin and

Marshall professor of English literature, argued for intellectually rigorous Jewish studies programs but feared that such arguments lacked the clout that identity politics packed: "Many figured that the best way for Jewish studies programs to gain access to the university was on the coattails of black studies and later, women's studies. Not surprisingly, the assets came with liabilities, as is now clear when the integrity of a discipline has been sold for a mess of potage ... The only reasonable response is to say no! and say it in thunder. No! to those Jews who think of Jewish studies programs as a place designed to make Yeshiva boys comfortable in their 'Jewishness.' No! to blacks who regard black studies programs as a place to indulge in romantic dreams of an Afrocentric separatism. No! to women's studies programs longer on consciousness raising than on intellectual rigor."[23]

Presentations at the annual Boston meetings of the Association of Jewish Studies, however, indicate a shift toward feminist issues and away from traditional areas such as the Bible and Jewish history. Professor Ruth Wisse, previously with McGill University's but now with Harvard's Jewish studies program, counted thirty-four papers on feminist issues, about 20 percent of all presentations, whereas biblical themes constituted 14 percent of presentations. Wisse characterized these papers as the triumph of the aggrieved and victimized, who are often ignorant of the larger historical situation in which anti-Semitism created powerless men and "dominant" women. Wisse concluded, "Jewish women owe it to their people to tell the truth about the power they traditionally wielded and the privileges they currently enjoy."[24]

Although changes in the intellectual core of Jewish studies scholarship is a source of disenchantment for Professor Wisse, other academics welcome the shift of Jewish studies from its traditional pedagogical and scholarly pursuits to topics such as the Jewish perspective on environmentalism and Jewish paganism. Participating faculty in some programs, such as New York University's, are highly specialized scholars with extensive training in numerous Semitic languages. Most programs, however, combine a range of courses from several departments, as does the Queens College program. At the Hebrew University Melton Centre for Jewish Education in the Diaspora, Professor Eilon Schwartz observed that "living in fear of paganism has ... not only exacted a heavy price on the Jewish relationship with nature. Feminists have argued that the cultural linking of nature with female has meant that a distancing of culture from nature is linked to a distancing of culture from its feminine components. Judaism's fear of paganism, therefore, has potentially led to a distancing of Judaism from feminine components."[25] The biblical narrative of the struggle of Judaism against paganism and nature gods is now understood, 4,000 years later, as an error to be overcome so that paganism and monotheism can join in reconstituting a new and improved Judaism.

Professor and Rabbi Howard Eilberg-Schwartz's personal and intellectual odyssey is informative. His publications include *The Savage in Judaism, God's Phallus and Other Problems for Men and Monotheism*, and an article against circumcision. Appointed head of the Jewish studies program at San Francisco State, he resigned a year later and also decided to leave academic life. He attributed his personal estrangement from Judaism to his acquired interest in gender theory.[26] His personal search for meaning, his pervasive introspection and distancing from Judaism, and his disenchantment with academic life could not be reconciled.

Identity politics that transform intellectual inquiry into therapeutic, self-discovery, and group-discovery endeavours, increasingly undermine the academy. *Diversity, pluralism, innovation*, and *inclusion*, words characterizing the ideals of university life, have become mantras on behalf of ideological agendas that narrow rather than broaden academic inquiry. Interdisciplinary studies frequently translate into nondisciplinarity – or knowing very little about the knowledge that informs the study of their respective disciplines. University students and faculty have to resist attempts to create institutions and curricula that reinforce and mirror group demographics, that attribute to individuals stereotypical roles and attitudes. Bernard Cooperman properly identified the academic's responsibility: "To stop students from uncritically accepting the nostalgic longings for an idealized past through which society promotes its own values ... I am not in the business of advocating nostalgia or a grandfather's religion."[27] A few years earlier, Allan Bloom wrote, "There is one simple rule for the university's activity: It need not concern itself with providing its students with experiences that are available in democratic society. They will have them in any event. It must provide them with experiences they cannot have there."[28]

The Jewish textual-intellectual tradition was a vehicle through which rabbis and sages imbibed and influenced the great books of Western culture – pagan, Moslem, and Christian. The fragmentation of the curriculum, ongoing threats to the tradition, and the decline of religious literacy, all make it difficult for more than a remnant of teachers and students to become educated. Would the following magnificent dialogue be possible in today's Jewish studies program or university, where rhetorical inclusivity has replaced intellectual inclusivity? Professor Leibowitz recounts an interesting exchange he had with Isaac Breuer:

Let me object, at the outset, to any attempt to explain anyone's views by where he comes from or who he is. I object as well to any attempt to distinguish between those who come from a milieu shaped by Western culture and those whose cultural and spiritual origins lie in Eastern Europe. I, too, belong to the Western world, although geographically speaking, I come from the East. I spent my childhood in Russia, but am familiar with Western science, philosophy, literature, and society not less than are the "Westerners." I recall a public debate more than thirty years ago between myself and the late Dr. Isaac Breuer, on the most interesting figures among religious Jews in the generation preceding ours, for whom I had great respect despite the considerable differences between our respective views. In that debate we drifted off to general philosophical problems, and though they were relevant to the issues that were close to our hearts, Judaism, Torah, and faith, they were fundamentally ontological and epistemological problems. Since Breuer argued persistently from the Jewish viewpoint, I said to him: "Dr. Breuer, why should we deceive ourselves? You know as well as I that in our treatment of philosophical questions both of us – who consider ourselves believing Jews, whose intention is to assume the yoke of the Kingdom of Heaven and the yoke of Torah and Mitzvoth – do not draw upon Jewish sources, but upon the atheistic antisemite Kant. We cannot do otherwise!" Breuer conceded at once that it would be impossible – even he could not do it – to discuss philosophic problems without recourse to Kant. Today, too, it is not the lack of familiarity with various aspects of European culture that created the rift between us. We are all equally steeped in Western culture.[29]

In addition to the intellectually rich, Jewish religious respect for Western thought, there existed a vital Jewish tradition that actively and enthusiastically devoured Western literature. Following the Second World War, a number of these secular, second-generation Jews ("New York Intellectuals") became prominent figures in American literary criticism. Although they often maintained a strong, scholarly interest in Jewish literature and politics, "they didn't consider it their job to lobby for opening up of the canon; they weren't in the business of getting Jewish writers like Sholem Aleichem and Isaac Babel on the syllabus. Some books you read on your own."[30] Lucy Dawidowicz spent her entire adult life studying and writing about the Holocaust. When she was asked if it should be taught in American public schools, she stated, "I'd feel a lot safer if they learned the meaning of the Constitution instead."[31]

Irving Howe once asked Jacob Glatstein, perhaps the most accomplished modernist Yiddish poet, "What does it mean to be a poet of an abandoned culture?" Glatstein perceptively replied, "It means that I have to be aware of Auden and Auden need never have heard of me."[32] As Jewish immigrants began to attend universities, they increasingly became interested in secular rather than Yiddish literature. The "potential readers of Glatstein became the actual readers of Eliot."[33] Steven J. Zipperstein, director of Stanford's Jewish studies program, believes this imbalance should be redressed. He states that Jewish studies programs need "to make someone who does not read Glatstein parochial."[34] This position might be relevant for students of Yiddish poetry, but should Glatstein bump an Auden from general poetry courses? Are the issues here sentimentality and ethnic affirmation? Should faculty throughout the university design curriculum predicated on random, particularistic identities that demand affirmation in student enrolment? Is there not a real danger that the contemporary enthusiasm for inclusion is more likely to result in the curriculum of exclusion and excision, where major texts and traditions are ignored because they do not suit private agendas or satisfy diversity and representational norms?

Salo Baron, a professor of history at Columbia, and Harry Wolfson, a professor of Near Eastern languages at Harvard, were the first two Jewish study appointments in America. They required their students to study the larger historical traditions informing their specialized Jewish interests. They did not wish to separate the "People of the Book" from the great books tradition of Western thought. A parallel is elegantly stated by the black Caribbean-American Marxist scholar, W.E.B. Du Bois: "I sit with Shakespeare and he winces not. Across the colour line I move arm and arm with Balzac and Dumas, where smiling men and welcoming women glide in gilded halls ... I summon Aristotle and Aurelius and what soul I will, and they come all graciously, with no scorn nor condescension. So, wed with Truth, I dwell above the veil."[35] If the intellectual breadth and understanding demonstrated by the likes of Soloveitchik, Baron, Wolfson, and James informed today's ethnic studies programs, we might have been spared their worst excesses.

Although group studies programs have proliferated in North America universities, it cannot be assumed that the financial and human resources expended to sustain them correspond to their intellectual importance. Although intended to broaden the curriculum and to expand the scope and breadth of knowledge about our collective past, they frequently fail to separate proper academic pursuits from therapeutic consciousness-raising. These programs might be the least diverse and least inclusive programs in the university.

Fearful and intimidated faculty and administrators are reluctant to question and oversee the quality of education received by their students. They are sensitive to the possibility that questions and criticisms of these programs might be interpreted as sexually, racially, and ethnically biased. The consequence of this passivity, withdrawal, and faculty and administrative complicity is a failure to oversee and appraise academic programs using the same criteria applied to other academic units.

To the degree the university community denies students opportunities to stretch beyond their own particular experiences and identities, students are patronized and victimized. For major segments of the university, education is informed by views that are properly described as an insidious pigmentation and chromosomal determinism. The desire to study and to understand our past as female, or black, or Jew, or any other designation is not the problem. The issue is how best to educate students. With regard to Jewish studies, I have attempted to outline both the distinctiveness and the inter-dependence of Jewish thought and Western culture. To the extent that a Jewish studies program pursues intellectual rather than identity issues, that it is open to all student and faculty with academic credentials, and that its curriculum and purpose is to study, not reconstruct and fabricate, the past, it is academically justified.

Major questions need to be addressed, however, about what constitutes Jewish culture, how such study should be structured, how its intellectual goals, chronological, and thematic focus should be defined, and who teaches what to whom. In a number of universities, the Jewish studies program is a department; in some instances, it does not hire permanent faculty but hires a director or coordinator who brings faculty together who share a teaching or research interest. There are Jewish studies programs that are highly struc-tured and focus on very specialized research interests; others try to be inno-vative, and instructors may be seen to lack scholarly credentials. In the Queens College controversy, academic pursuits came into conflict with com-munity concerns, but the conflict was also about defining a field, a curricu-lum, and a faculty.

For Jewish studies to succeed, it must distinguish between the needs of undergraduate students who move on to other pursuits, the requirements of its very small number of graduate students, and the research interests of its professors, which may or may not be relevant to either group of stu-dents. Will students graduating from an interdisciplinary Jewish studies program be better served than they would be taking relevant courses in traditional disciplines? Will students studying the Bible, Jewish history and texts, Yiddish and Hebrew literature, or other disciplines that inform the Jewish tradition be exposed to non-Jewish courses in the discipline that provide the necessary context for their more particular interests? Through-out the ages, Judaism – its religion, culture, and history – has been shaped by rabbis, sages, and scholars. Their genius extended well beyond their own faith.

## Notes

1 Letter to the editor, *Forward*, 2 August 1996, 6.
2 Mohamad Bazzi, "After Prof Quits, Questions Raised," *Newsday*, 17 July 1996, A03.
3 Courtney Leatherman, "Head of Jewish Studies at Queens College, Quits," *Chronicle of Higher Education*, 6 July 1996, A18.
4 Eric J. Greenberg, "The Dirty Little Secret about Jewish Studies: Queens College Flap," *Jewish Week*, 2 August 1996, PG.
5 Letter to the editor, *New York Times*, 20 July 1996.
6 YIVO is the Yiddish acronym for Yiddisher Visenshaftlikher Institut, translated in English as the Institute for Jewish Research.
7 Allan Nadler, "The Question of Quality at Queens," *Forward*, 26 July 1996, 7.

8 Bernard D. Cooperman, "Jewish Studies and Jewish Identity: Some Implications of Secularizing Torah," *Judaism* 432 (1993): 238.
9 Letter to the editor, "Seattle's Success," *Forward,* 2 August 1996, 6.
10 Mohamad Bazzi, "'Bigotry' Pushes Prof to Resign/College Assailed for Picking Non-Jew," *Newsday,* 16 July 1996, A03.
11 Greenberg, PG. The same quotation also appears in Marilyn Henry's article in the 18 July *Jerusalem Post,* 12.
12 Letter to the editor, *New York Times,* 17 July 1996.
13 Letter to the editor, *New York Times,* 20 July 1996.
14 Leatherman, A18.
15 Letter to the editor, *Forward,* 2 August 1996.
16 Letter to the editor, *Forward,* 2 August 1996.
17 Jonathan Mahler, "Charges of Bigotry at Queens Rattles through Ivory Tower," *Forward,* 19 July 1996.
18 Letter to the editor, *New York Times,* 17 July 1996.
19 Arthur Hertzberg, "Let's Abolish Jewish Studies Departments," *Jewish Week,* 26 July 1996, PG.
20 *Washington Post,* 18 July 1996, 18.
21 Daphne Patai and Noretta Koertge, *Professing Feminism* (New York: Basic Books, 1994), xix. Christine Hoff Sommers notes that "much of what students learn in women's studies classes is not disciplined scholarship but feminist ideology." See *Who Stole Feminism* (New York: Simon and Schuster, 1994), 51.
22 Dinesh D'Souza, *Illiberal Education* (New York: Free Press, 1991), 226. For example, Glenn Loury transferred from Harvard University's Afro-American studies to its Kennedy School of Government.
23 Sanford Pinsker, "Queens College Firing – Ethnic Studies in a Jewish Pickle," *MetroWest Jewish News,* 8 August 1996, PG.
24 Ruth Wisse, "The Feminist Mystery," *Jerusalem Report,* 9 January 1992, 140.
25 Eilon Schwartz, "Judaism and Nature: Theological and Moral Issues to Consider While Renegotiating a Jewish Relationship to the Natural World," *Judaism* 44 (1995): 441.
26 Howard Eilberg-Schwartz, "This Alien Thing That Is My Inheritance," *Judaism* 44 (1995): 432.
27 Cooperman, 234.
28 Alan Bloom, *The Closing of the American Mind* (New York: Simon and Schuster, 1987), 256.
29 Yeshayahu Leibowitz, *Judaism, Human Values and the Jewish State,* ed. Eliezer Goldman, 106-107 (Cambridge: Harvard University Press, 1992). Soloveitchik, recognizing Kant's influence as well, argued for a new Jewish philosophy, separate from Jewish medieval philosophy, which he saw as "rooted in ancient Greek and medieval Arabic thought." See Rabbi Joseph B. Soloveitchik, *The Halakhic Mind* (New York: Seth Press, 1986), 100.
30 James Atlas, *Battle of the Books* (New York: W.W. Norton and Company, 1992), 108.
31 Richard Bernstein, *Dictatorship of Virtue* (New York: Alfred A. Knopf, 1994), 285.
32 Irving Howe, *World of Our Fathers* (New York: Harcourt Brace Jovanovich, 1974), 452.
33 Howe, p. 441.
34 Steven J. Zipperstein, "Home Again?" *Judaism* 44 (1995): 436.
35 Arthur M. Schlesinger Jr., *The Disuniting of America* (New York: W.W. Norton and Company, 1992), 91.

# 12
# Are Course Evaluations a Threat to Academic Freedom?
*Stanley Coren*

Virtually all members of the academic community agree that racist or sexist activities should be eliminated. This agreement probably explains the proliferation of committees and codes to monitor such behaviours. But it is the practical matter of *how* classroom activities are to be monitored to detect possible racist and sexist behaviours that concerns me. Specifically, we must ask, "Where and how is the evidence being obtained to support charges of racism or sexism on the part of faculty?" We can all agree that if the data used as evidence of racist or sexist actions are not valid and reliable, then any subsequent conclusions based on that data are questionable. Unfortunately, there are reasons to believe data from the most commonly used source of such information in universities may be both flawed and biased.

To determine whether there is racism and sexism in the classroom, we need information about what faculty members say and do during lectures and other course-related activities. Despite the fact that scientific methods and the accuracy of measurement procedures are a matter of study in many college courses, when it comes to gathering data about the university and its personnel, the design of data collection is often driven more by convenience and economy than by concerns for scientific validity. One example of this tendency is the familiar use of standardized, pencil-and-paper evaluations of instructors and courses. These evaluations are usually completed by students at the end of each term. The data are quickly and inexpensively obtained. It is frequently the major (and sometimes the only) information used to determine the quality of a faculty member's teaching.

Most faculty think very little about such evaluations; they tend to look on them as a routine requirement of their jobs, not much different from placing orders for textbooks or submitting final grades to the registrar's office. Few faculty members question the results obtained from such evaluations. After all, who better than the student knows whether the teacher taught well? Remember that students are the people who actually heard the lectures, read the textbooks, took the exams, and so forth. Furthermore, at face value, the rating procedures appear scientific. Using a 1 to 5 numerical scale, students simply check off responses to questions about the course and the instructor. These forms are then scored and turned into numbers. Once this calculation is done, we see that Professor Smith has a mean teaching rating of 3.8, which is obviously less than that of Professor Jones, whose rating is 4.6 out of a possible 5: irrefutable proof that Professor Jones is the superior teacher.

Unfortunately, just because a set of ratings is displayed in numerical form and shown as means, standard deviations, or distributions of scores does not guarantee scientific validity. Validity depends on the accuracy of the student judgments used to generate those numbers in the first place. Some of the items on most course evaluations seem easy for students to answer validly. Certainly, students should be able to provide accurate information when asked "Was the instructor usually on time?" or "Were course requirements clearly stated?" or "Did the instructor provide time to answer questions?" or "Were the lectures clear and well organized?" Yet there are other questions on many course evaluation forms where a reasonable person might doubt the students' competence to provide valid information. How about "Did the instructor demonstrate a clear understanding of the material?" or "Was the material covered in the course appropriate?" These two questions cannot be validly answered by students. Both presuppose prior knowledge and understanding of the substantive material from which the course content was drawn as well as an understanding of how that content relates to other aspects of the discipline. Obviously, students taking an introductory course won't have this information. Remember that experts in any field often have very different views about which course material is appropriate for inclusion – isn't that why there are so many differences among textbooks purporting to cover the same material?

The real problem, however, appears when we turn to the "hot" issues associated with political and cultural attitudes. Because it is convenient to do so, many academic institutions have added course evaluation items designed to monitor the acceptability of faculty behaviour in the classroom. Now students are asked to provide their perceptions of any apparent prejudice on the part of their instructors. Items include such questions as "Did the instructor ever make comments or display attitudes that could be construed as being sexist?" or "Did the instructor ever use language or make comments that were demeaning to members of certain racial groups?" Administrators argue that such items help monitor racism and sexism in the classroom. The way this procedure should work is clear. If too many students claim an instructor displays racist or sexist attitudes, then the instructor can be warned or the case can be referred to the appropriate antiharassment committee for disciplinary action. No question about the actual validity of such items is ever raised: data collection is just a matter of expedience.

What could be simpler than adding a few questions to the existing standard form? Faculty members already accustomed to periodic evaluation by students are unlikely to complain. To raise the issue of the validity of the items suggests that the complaining faculty members know that they are guilty of the unwholesome behaviours targeted by such questions, and their comments indicate that they fear being caught.

Yet if blameless faculty members are thinking clearly, they should be concerned about such items. Perhaps a history lesson will help us see why. Some people reading this chapter may be old enough to remember that student evaluations were a product of the stormy political conditions of the sixties. Campus life was punctuated with noisy meetings convened by rebellious students with long lists of demands. Just about every one of these lists contained a demand for standardized evaluations of courses and instructors. This demand, like many others, was supported with phrases and slogans such as "Power to the students" or "Universities should be democracies." As every student at that time knew, the real agenda was that the students wanted to dictate not only *how* they were taught but also *what* they were taught. Implementing the evaluations and taking their results seriously would give students political leverage.

This was one fight that the students won. Their goals were quickly realized. Faculty members and even whole academic departments responded to student evaluations by altering their courses. The most vulnerable faculty members, such as those who were untenured and felt that negative teaching evaluations might cost them their jobs, often responded by anticipating negative criticism and changing course content and structure in a preemptive surrender to student criticism.

As expected, course evaluations also gave students tremendous political power. Part of this power came from the fact that students were guaranteed anonymity for their course ratings. Such anonymity seems like a sensible protection from faculty retaliation. Unfortunately, that same anonymity left instructors in an extremely vulnerable position. Given the fact that filling out a course evaluation form is a completely unattributable act, this rating process could be used in an abusive or capricious manner. There was no way to ensure student responsibility during the evaluation process. Students could give any rating that they chose. The act was unchallengeable; the actor untraceable. Faculty members couldn't appeal, ask for justification, or demand evidence supporting judgments about their classroom behaviour. For the students filling in the rating form, there were no personal consequences for negligent, false, or malicious misrepresentations. Apparently, North American colleges decided that students were inherently trustworthy, and any statement they made on course evaluations should be accepted at face value.

Someone might protest that I am unduly cynical, for students would have no reason to falsify evaluations. But history proves otherwise: evaluations can and have been used to impose political views on instructors and to punish those whose viewpoints deviate from those desired by students. There is the case of a senior faculty member in one university who had always received good teaching ratings. One year, this faculty member was denied a merit-based pay increase because his course evaluations had plummeted to an exceedingly low level. Many of his colleagues suspected that the real reason for his low ratings had nothing to do with his teaching abilities but rather was the result of the fact that he took an unpopular stand on a campus political issue. The next semester an article appeared in the campus newspaper bragging that students had deliberately biased his course evaluations. Local campus policy required that course evaluations be done on the last day of class, so it was easy for students who were not registered in the course to show up on that day to fill in negative ratings. That this campus newspaper story was probably true seems to be supported by the fact that the course ratings were based on 184 student evaluation forms submitted, yet only 151 students were officially registered in the course. The writer of the article went on to say that this tactic was justifiable and useful, and ought to be employed when dealing with other faculty members and other political issues.

There is little protection against this kind of action. Universities have given so much trust and responsibility to students in this area that it would be unheard of to challenge any student's right to fill in a rating form. Furthermore, the anonymity of student responses ensures that they will never be called on to justify their ratings. Was the university's confidence in student course evaluations shaken by the previously described event? Apparently not. The administration's only response to this obvious travesty was the publication of a letter pointing out to students that course evaluations were taken seriously by the university, and students were urged not to do this sort of thing in the future. (See Coren 1998 for a full discussion of this and similar cases.)

Although I do not know how to do so, let's pretend that we could eliminate the use of course ratings as a method of exerting political pressure. Even under these circumstances, any competent social psychologist can tell us we cannot rely on the validity of student evaluations to tell us about racist or sexist behaviours in the classroom.

Two very well known psychological processes can easily predict bias in student evaluations of faculty members. The first is the psychological predisposition commonly called the *fundamental attribution* error. It predicts that students may be unable to separate the message from the messenger when evaluating their perception of prejudice in the classroom. Just about every textbook on social psychology presents examples of the fundamental attribution error. One empirical demonstration comes from a study by Jones and Harris (1967). They had participants in an experiment read a speech that either supported or attacked Fidel Castro. There were two experimental conditions. In the first, participants were told that the person who wrote the speech decided which political position to support. In the second condition, participants were told that the person who wrote the essay had no choice about the position for which he or she was to argue: the person was simply assigned a side to champion. Obviously, in the first condition a reasonable person would conclude that if people could choose to argue for a side, then they would choose the position they believed in. In the second case, however, the essay itself said nothing about the actual beliefs of the writer.

In spite of the fact that participants in this study knew that the writer in the second condition had no choice as to the position he or she advocated, participants still believed that the writer's actual beliefs were in agreement with the position supported. This finding has been repeated many times. It makes no difference if the topic being written or spoken about is nuclear power, drug laws, the death penalty, lifestyles, or sex differences. Even with full knowledge that writers had no choice in the position they supported, readers still believe that the writers' arguments truly reflect their personal beliefs and desires.

When we move from the social psychology laboratory to the real world, we can predict that the fundamental attribution error will affect the validity of student evaluations in many courses. Psychologists and other behavioural scientists who teach courses containing material on individual differences often find themselves presenting research findings that are politically unpopular in today's social climate. Typically, segments of most introductory psychology courses deal with individual and group differences in intelligence and mental abilities. An honest treatment of this material requires that evidence be presented indicating that both environmental and genetic factors determine intelligence. This requirement pops open the Pandora's box containing one of the most inflammatory issues in society today; namely, whether genetic factors determine racial differences in intelligence. The evidence is clear that various races score better or worse on standard intelligence tests. Most researchers and most textbooks agree that although environmental factors are important in determining these patterns of scores, genetic contributions cannot be ignored because a wealth of animal and human twin data supports genetic contributions to mental abilities (for example, Plomin 1989). Neither of these conclusions is popular with students who view as racist any conclusion of genetic differences in abilities, let alone any possibility of racial differences in performance.

An equally incendiary research area is possible sex differences in mental abilities. Again, the research literature is clear: there are systematic differences in the pattern of abilities displayed by males and females on standardized tests. Some differences may be environmental and may reflect differences in the socialization of males and females. Other ability differences between the sexes appear to be genetically controlled, a direct consequence of hormonal, neurological, and brain structure differences between men and women. The conscientious lecturer interested in presenting the full picture must discuss these physical differences as well as environmental, cultural, and socialization factors (for example, Halpern 1992).

Is it possible for the students to separate objectively presented scientific data from their perception of the instructor's attitudes? The fundamental attribution error suggests that this outcome is unlikely, a conclusion supported by data from an empirical study I conducted (Coren 1993). I gave a group of 198 first-year university students this scenario: "Professor X gives a lecture about intelligence. In it, he describes some evidence that biological factors, such as genes, affect intelligence. He suggests that although culture and experience are important in determining scores on intelligence tests, genetic factors can explain some portion of the difference in IQ scores obtained when different races take intelligence tests." Note that although Professor X suggests that there is a genetic contribution to intelligence, he also acknowledges contributions from culture and environment. His final conclusion is cautious, suggesting that the genetic contribution to intelligence might account for "some portion" of the differences observed in IQ scores between the races.

When asked what the professor's motives might have been for presenting this material, nearly one out of every four of the students (24 percent of the respondents) specifically mentioned "racist," "racism," or notions of "racial superiority" as motivating factors. Thus, as would be predicted by the fundamental attribution error, the very discussion of genetic and racial differences in intelligence, at least if the conclusion is that such differences exist, renders the lecturer a racist in the minds of nearly one-quarter of the students.

I gave the group another example involving a lecture on sex differences: "Professor Z gives a lecture about sex differences. In it, he notes evidence that males consistently score better than females in spatial and mathematical tests. He suggests that while societal and environmental contributions should not be ignored, some portion of these sex differences in ability may be the result of genetic factors or differences in the brain structure of males and females." Despite Professor Z's statement that social and environmental factors may contribute to the observed sex differences and the cautious conclusion that "some portion" of these differences "may" be the result of physiological or genetic differences between males and females, the students still conclude that he is sexist. In this case, 31 percent of the students mentioned "sexist," "sexism," "antiwomen," "putting women down," or equivalents as the primary motivation behind Professor Z's lecture.

These results are very distressing. As predicted by the fundamental attribution error, students interpret information that they don't like or don't want to be true as a reflection of the instructor's personal views and attitudes. To be told that women score more poorly on spatial tests is thus sufficient to brand the speaker as hostile to women. The lecturer pointing out that data published in the research literature force these conclusions on us will not affect the students' view of the instructor. Remember that experiments on this issue demonstrate that even telling people that a random selection determined the positions that people were forced to support did not prevent observers from concluding that the arguments reflected personal convictions.

Ultimately, a second problem may even more powerfully negate the validity of student evaluations on these sensitive political issues. This problem has to do with a phenomenon that psychologists refer to as *halo effects*, which means that if you like some aspects of a person, then you will tend to view everything that person says or does in a positive light. Conversely, if you dislike a person, you will tend to judge everything about that person in a negative light.

Halo effects influence interpersonal judgments. For instance, Nisbett and Wilson (1977) found that experimental subjects rated a person who acted in a cold, nasty manner not only as cold and negative but also as less physically attractive than a person who acted in a warm, outgoing manner. Such a person may also be seen as less intelligent, lazy, or even bigoted. In the context of student evaluation, the halo effect suggests that poor instructors, who may be disliked because their teaching is boring or disorganized, are also likely be rated lower on nonpedagogical, political items. Halo effects would lead us to expect that the negative feelings held by the student evaluator on any one factor could result in a negative bias on every other rating factor in a teaching survey, including racism and sexism.

Fortuitously, an opportunity to test this prediction from the halo effect presented itself (see Coren 1998). My department recently modified its teaching evaluation form to introduce three nonteaching questions: one asked about racism, another about sexism, and the third about cultural sensitivity. This revision allowed me to study student evaluations of particular faculty members. My database contained 248 evaluation forms submitted to the department as part of our annual evaluation process. They were volunteered by one instructor of introductory psychology. It is extremely important to limit the data to one instructor because differences between instructors may exist in terms of racism or sexism. It is also important to limit the data to a single course because differences in course content might confound results by eliciting different degrees of the fundamental attribution error. Limiting the data to one course and one instructor means that the lectures and course performance every student is evaluating are constant.

Evidence for a halo effect in student ratings would be a finding that the ratings for course quality and for political and social content will not be independent. Simply put, those students who do not like the instructor or the course should be more likely to label the instructor as racist, sexist, and culturally biased, while the students who like the instructor should be more likely to respond with favourable ratings on these politically sensitive items. As Table 1 shows, the results of my analysis showed a frighteningly strong halo effect. Every one of the tabled correlations is significant at $p < .001$ or better. The overall pattern is clear, demonstrating a high correlation between items explicitly designed to measure classroom performance and items designed to measure political climate in the classroom: students with an unfavourable opinion of the course are predisposed to accuse the instructor of sexism, racism, and cultural insensitivity.

*Table 1*

**Correlations between evaluations on teaching competency and questions about the social and political attitudes of the instructor**

| Teaching questionnaire items assessing instructor competence | Social/political attitude questions | | |
| --- | --- | --- | --- |
| | Is the instructor racist? | Is the instructor sexist? | Does the instructor show cultural bias? |
| Encouraged participation | −.415 | −.482 | −.342 |
| Instructor well prepared | −.403 | −.419 | −.382 |
| Available in office hours | −.380 | −.383 | −.462 |
| Used practical applications | −.443 | −.392 | −.454 |
| Too high-level communication | .517 | .474 | .453 |
| Time poorly used | .476 | .500 | .442 |
| Encouraged thinking | −.428 | −.445 | −.483 |
| Poorly organized | .538 | .541 | .471 |
| Answered questions | −.514 | −.385 | −.652 |
| Demonstrated knowledge | −.454 | −.416 | −.552 |
| Raised student interest | −.442 | −.464 | −.463 |
| Instructor not interested | .416 | .398 | .434 |
| Course requirements clear | −.357 | −.352 | −.324 |
| Textbook good | −.481 | −.478 | −.279 |

*Notes:* These values are based on introductory psychology evaluation forms from a sample of 248 students, all of whom were evaluating the same instructor. All correlations shown are significant at $p < 0.001$.

Think about the implications of these findings. These results say that not being available at office hours, not encouraging student participation, not explaining course requirements clearly, not showing interest in the subject matter, or even using a difficult or boring textbook will result in the instructor not only being rated as a bad teacher but also being indicted as a sexist or racist. Remember that all of the responses analyzed were from the same instructor, which means that some appealing alternatives that might explain this halo effect, such as the suggestion that racist instructors might also be bad teachers, are not possible. Remember, too, that these results are based on ratings for a course by students who knew that the ratings might have a direct influence on the instructor's career.

Although at first glance it may not be obvious, inherent in this discussion of the influence of halo effects on student ratings is an attack on academic standards. Which factor is most likely to cast a positive glow or a negative pallor on a student's evaluation of a course? Listen to student conversations, and it is clear that in their eyes the best instructors are those who give them good grades; the worst are those who give them bad grades. The evidence on halo effects then predicts that the severity of grading may affect the evaluation of the instructors' teaching ability and their political sensitivity.

To test whether grades influence the halo effect found in Table 1, I obtained access to the department's annual student evaluations for certain large enrolment courses. On our course assessment forms, each item uses a five-point scale that runs from strongly agree to strongly disagree. For the purposes of analysis, I shall simply dichotomize this data. Thus students who say they agree or strongly agree that the instructor made racist comments will be classified as seeing a problem of racism in the classroom; a similar dichotomization will be made for ratings of sexism. Such a scoring system allows us to quickly see the effects of grades on student evaluations of the political climate in the classroom.

First, I looked at two sections of a course taught by the same instructor, using the same textbook, in two successive years. Enrolments for the two sections were 274 and 271 students. In this instance, the instructor chose not to scale the course grades to some arbitrary grade distribution but simply added the scores across the examinations to provide a final grade. As often happens when grades are not scaled, there is a difference in the class averages for the two years: the better class averaged 71 percent and the poorer class averaged 64 percent. These differences probably reflect random variation in student ability, which causes differences in the range of grades across sections. Even though the course evaluations are filled out before the release of final grades, most students have a reasonable idea about their final grade based on the three or four exams they have already taken in the course. If grades produce a halo in students' minds, then we should also

*Figure 1*

**Student ratings of instructor racism and sexism for an instructor who taught two sections of the same course, using the same textbook, in successive years, plotted as a function of grade average for the section**

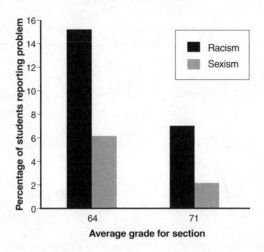

find the halo effect operating on students' evaluations of the instructor's racism and sexism. The data are shown in Figure 1.

As expected from considerations of the halo effect, the mean grade differences resulted in systematic differences in the students' ratings of the instructor's racist and sexist tendencies. In the poorer class, students were more than twice as likely to rate the instructor as sexist (15 percent compared to 7 percent) and three times as likely to rate the instructor as racist (6 percent compared to 2 percent). In both cases, these differences are statistically significant ($z = 2.98$, $p < .01$ for sexism, and $z = 2.38$, $p < .05$ for racism).

Although these data seem to provide powerful evidence that halo effects bias ratings, a sceptic might explain this conclusion by appealing to situational differences. Perhaps during that second, low-graded year, the instructor was having a bad time. Perhaps his marriage was falling apart, which made him more cynical about women and hence more likely to utter sexist remarks in the classroom, or perhaps his property values had been negatively influenced by ethnic change in the demographics of his neighbourhood, which might cause him to make racist comments. Because we can't know for sure, let us consider another instructor in a more controlled classroom situation.

For the next analysis, I was fortunate to obtain course evaluations from an instructor who taught two large sections of the same course during the same year (enrolments were 272 and 269 students). The sections were taught back-to-back in the same auditorium and used the same textbook. The instructor describes the situation this way:

> The lectures were virtually identical. I used the same slides and transparencies in the same sequence. I pointed out to the students that they could sit in on either section and they would get the same material. A lot of students said that they liked that flexibility and often changed which lecture they came to in order to accommodate other aspects of their schedule or their day-to-day moods. One student decided to sit through both lectures one morning. He came up to me afterwards to tell me that not only was the course content the same, but also I had used the same jokes and the same "off the cuff" comments in the two lectures.

Although the course material was the same, the grades were not. This instructor used identical multiple-choice examinations in both sections (for security, the order of the questions and response alternatives were scrambled). When he separated the grades by sections, however, there was a large difference in class averages: one section scored a mean of 72 percent and the

*Figure 2*

**Student ratings of instructor racism and sexism for an instructor who taught two sections of the same course, back-to-back in the same year, using the same textbook and audiovisual aids, plotted as a function of grade average for the section**

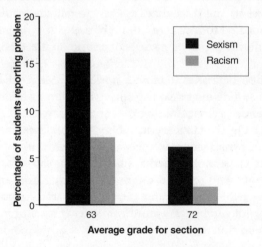

other section scored 63 percent for their final grade. As can be seen from Figure 2, there is also a large difference between the two sections in the students' reports that the instructor had a problem with racism and sexism.

The figure clearly shows the same halo effects that we have now come to expect, giving a systematic bias to the instructor's ratings on racism and sexism consistent with the mean course grades. In the lower-scoring class, the instructor is 2.5 times more likely to be rated as sexist (16 percent compared to 6 percent) and also more than three times more likely to be called racist (7 percent compared to 2 percent). Again, these differences achieve conventionally accepted levels of statistical significance ($z = 3.71$, $p < .001$ for sexism, and $z = 2.80$, $p < .01$ for racism). These results clearly indicate that an instructor who grades more harshly is setting up a negative halo effect that will influence every aspect of the students' evaluation of the course and of the faculty member's performance, including politically sensitive questions about racist and sexist comments in the classroom.

Those individuals who are committed to standardized student rating forms and who feel that course evaluations ought to include assessment of faculty attitudes with respect to political, racial, and cultural issues are often not swayed by empirical data such as those presented here. Their response is to argue that the biases we have seen in this data arise because of problems with the particular measurement device or rating form administered to the students, not with the general concept of course evaluation itself. These individuals contend that specific procedures can eliminate bias associated with the attribution and halo effects. They usually suggest that phrasing questions differently – in a more balanced manner – will suffice. They claim that it should be possible to present politically sensitive items so that students become aware of the potential for judgmental errors and avoid them in their evaluations.

Actually, all of the data that I have used as examples here have come from a student evaluation form where a concerted attempt was made to minimize the psychological preconceptions that show up as attribution errors or halos. When the politically sensitive items that we have been looking at were added to the course evaluation forms, a number of faculty members raised concerns that students could not, or would not, make distinctions between academic content and political content. We were assured by those who favoured inclusion of such "classroom climate questions" that students did have the ability to separate matters of attitude from those of content. Moreover, the designers of the questionnaire went to special lengths in their response to those who objected to the controversial question. First, they boxed the three politically sensitive questions so that they would stand out from the others. Next, they provided the following brief introductory paragraph: "The following three statements are to be answered on the basis of *how* the instructor has presented the material in this course. *Do not* answer them on the basis of the course content or the instructor's choice of topics. The objective, scientific examination of such issues as race and gender differences in psychological traits and behaviour is a legitimate part of the curriculum in some psychology courses and should not be regarded as demeaning to any group."

The presumption was that the inclusion of such a paragraph, along with the physical separation and boxing of the political items, would offset the fundamental attribution error, and demarcating these items as special and different would reduce the halo effect. Because the pattern of correlations in Table 1 involved answering these boxed questions after reading the caution, the halo effect was clearly not eliminated by this action.

That the fundamental attribution error is not eliminated by the printed disclaimer can be seen by looking at the back of the evaluation form, where "Other Comments" allows students to expand on their responses. One evaluation form contained the student comment "Telling the class that girls don't do as well as boys in math and geometry was uncalled for. I still intend to get a degree in engineering and will do it to spite sexists like you!" It is not surprising that this evaluation form also contained a rating suggesting that the instructor was extremely sexist. From this same class, however, we also get the comment "I really liked the fact that you pointed out that women have better verbal skills then [sic] men. I want to be a writer and appreciate professors like you who are so supportive to women." This comment was accompanied by a rating indicating that the instructor was not sexist at all. Because both facts appeared in the same lecture on intelligence, this pair of comments, which confuse the instructor's attitudes and beliefs with the experimental data presented, indicates selective perception accompanied by the fundamental attribution error.

The vice president of a major university heard me present these data at a conference. He commented, "There is already a well-established tradition that accepts the use of student evaluations as a means of monitoring faculty teaching performance. In the current political climate, we need to look at how sex and race issues are dealt with by instructors. You demonstrate that student ratings are biased, and I accept that. On the other hand, you offer nothing to use in their place. I feel that if student ratings are all that we have to measure racism and sexism on campus, then that is what we will have to use."

I was saddened but not surprised. His argument is similar to that given by early medical practitioners who were faced with evidence that medicinal bleeding and the administration of large doses of mercury not only did not cure infectious diseases but also may well have hastened, or even caused, the deaths of patients. In those days before antibiotics, physicians argued that such procedures were the only treatments available, so in the absence of anything else to prescribe, they continued to use those therapies despite the lack of evidence to support their effectiveness. We now know that such procedures so weakened the immune systems of patients that they often succumbed to diseases that their bodies could have fought successfully had they been left untreated by their physicians.

For now, I am unable to propose a replacement for student evaluations. However, we must recognize that student evaluations do not provide unbiased data on the racism and sexism of instructors. The analyses presented here indicate what any social psychologist might have been able to predict from already published experimental data; namely, student evaluations are tainted by both the fundamental attribution error and the halo effect. If students don't like what an instructor says about a group, position, or belief with which they identify, then we know that students may perceive the instructor as having hostile and discriminatory motivations and attitudes. If students do not like an instructor's teaching style, class organization, or textbook, then given the opportunity, they may label that instructor as racist, sexist, and culturally biased. If all you have to evaluate instructor performance are student course evaluations, then a faculty member who lacks charisma, gives difficult exams, and is disorganized in the classroom may appear racist and sexist. Furthermore, based on student evaluations, if an instructor presents scientifically valid information about race or sex differences and dares to include some politically unpopular conclusions, then some students will conclude that the faculty member is polluting the classroom with racism and sexism.

If we are looking for insights into the political climate in the classroom, there is clear evidence that information gathered from student evaluations is often biased and inaccurate. The issue of racism and sexism in the classroom is too important to be left to assessments based on something as demonstrably flawed and confounded as simple tabulations of responses to items included on student course evaluation forms. As the humorist Josh Billings once quipped, "Tez better to know nothin' than to know what ain't so."

**References**
Coren, S. 1993. When Teaching Is Evaluated on Political Grounds." *Academic Questions* 6: 73-9.
–. 1998. "Student Evaluations of an Instructor's Racism and Sexism: Truth or Expedience?" *Ethics and Behavior* 8: 201-13.
Halpern, D.F. 1992. *Sex Differences in Cognitive Abilities*. Hillsdale, NJ: Erlbaum.
Jones, E.E., and V.A. Harris. 1967. "The Attribution of Attitudes." *Journal of Personality and Social Psychology* 3: 1-24.
Nisbett, R.W., and T.D. Wilson. 1977. "The Halo Effect: Evidence of Unconscious Alteration of Judgements." *Journal of Personality and Social Psychology* 35: 250-6.
Plomin, R. 1989. "Environment and Genes: Determinants of Behavior." *American Psychologist* 44: 105-11.

# Part 4
# Theoretical and Practical Challenges to the Inclusive University

# 13
# Meeting the Challenge of Religious Fundamentalism: How Far Do Liberal Principles of Tolerance Go?
*Diane Dyson*

This is the story of a harassment complaint in which I participated at a Canadian university. The case arises out of my background as a student advocate. Because of my participation in the case, I might easily be accused of some partisanship. However, I have tried to be fair and balanced in my account. Despite my position in the middle of the complaint, I think an examination of the case is valuable. It will show that there are no right answers to the questions posed. The purpose of this exploration is to reveal *how* a university would or could respond to such a case, rather than how *this* particular complaint was resolved. Reliance on memory, personal notes, and subsequent interviews with key participants form the basis of this account. Identifying characteristics of the university or individuals involved have been deleted or changed to maintain anonymity.

In the memory of bureaucrats at the university, no student had ever won an academic appeal or harassment case on the grounds of ethno-cultural or racial prejudice, despite the fact that the grounds for such complaints are enshrined in policy. This enigma has pulled at me, demanding answers as to how difference is constructed and enacted within the academy. This case is the sticky stuff of institutional life, where policy is tested against realities. It also offers insights into a predicament of policy into which universities have bound themselves.

A Christian fundamentalist student, who was enrolled in a required sociology class, lodged a complaint under the university harassment prevention policy on the ground of ethnicity. This ground is defined by the policy to include discrimination on the basis of religion. Her specific complaint arose out of what she called the excessive use of profanity and blasphemy by the professor. Over twelve weeks and forty-five hours of class time, the student meticulously catalogued more than 130 expletives used by the professor. In addition, the student listed about a dozen particular instances where she felt that Christianity, Christians, or the Bible had been singled out and held up for ridicule. The student contended that all these actions on the part of the professor were purposeful and intended to create an intimidating and poisoned environment for her. During the term, the student approached the departmental assistant and chair with her complaints. Although the atmosphere in the classroom eased temporarily, the professor commented to the class that his actions were being monitored. Shortly thereafter, the professor resumed his previous course of comment and action.

The student then decided to pursue a formal harassment complaint. The teaching department denied the complaint at the first level. The student chose to pursue it further, and the faculty dean was asked to arbitrate. Interviews with the complainant and respondent ensued. Each was asked to produce witnesses in support of their case and confidential transcripts were made of all these sessions.

In response to the complaint, the professor defended both the style and the content of his comments. He claimed that his teaching style, which includes frequent swearing, was meant to shake students out of the complacency of their early-life belief systems so that they might understand other concepts. He held that questioning of particular religious beliefs was a vital part of the normal discourse of his scholarly discipline. Furthermore, the professor produced students from the class – none of whom claim the same religious background as the complainant – who enthusiastically supported his teaching methods. Any action against his position by the university would, he argued, be seen as an infringement of his academic freedom, which was defended by the harassment policy. He also threatened to respond to any further appeal by the student with his own complaint of frivolous action. The dean was left to consider the complaint.

Let us first examine the theoretical frameworks of this case, commencing with the liberal ideal of education. Liberalism assumes publicly funded education serves two broad purposes. The first, the utilitarian function, shapes students "to function effectively in their social worlds" (Vine 1992: 169). This includes, at the postsecondary level, occupational training and granting of credentials for the workplace. This function has gained increasing importance as colleges and universities educate an increasing number and proportion of citizens. The second function of education is related to the liberal arts tradition of the academy: the university helps students to "develop their potential to identify and achieve a fulfilled life" (Vine 1992: 169). Within higher education, this has historically meant an emphasis on developing a mental agility "to see things as they are, to go right to the point, to disentangle a skein of thought, to detect what is sophistical, and to discard what is irrelevant" (Newman 1852: 154). This latter function, of seeking a truth, has been the source of much controversy in recent decades.

The university academic culture can also be viewed as a community that enacts moral prescriptives through policy to regulate the behaviour of its own members. To Vine, the term/expression *"moral system* of any social group" can be broadly defined as "the collective regulation of *social conflicts of interest* ... among *ingroup members"* (1992: 183-4). As a code of conduct, a university's harassment prevention policy may therefore be seen as evidence of a moral system that values certain behaviours over others.

A central and predominant value within the academy is the principle of academic freedom. Essentially, it is freedom of inquiry, a tradition which sprang from the schools of Ancient Greece and was guarded in Medieval Europe, revived within the German research institutes, and succoured within American universities. This historical legacy of the Socratic method of inquiry has structured our university traditions, including the institutional drive for knowledge. Transplanted from its European roots, the notion of academic freedom has meant the freedom for the scholar "to follow an argument," as Socrates urged, "whithersoever it may lead" (Brubacher 1977: 42). Through open questioning, where nothing is held as sacred, scholars are "enabled to approach problematic human predicaments more adequately than would otherwise have been possible" (Pekarsky 1994: 120). In addition to being an end in itself, the pursuit of knowledge through Socratic dialogue ostensibly provides direct benefits for those engaged in the process. Such an education "will stimulate the development of the student's beliefs in the direction of greater generality, differentiation and overall coherence" (Pekarsky 1994: 119-20). However, this "good" as defined by the academy rests on several assumptions that deserve closer analysis.

Part of the foundation of the academy is the assumption of rational action; that is, the belief that once individuals are shown the irrationality of a belief, they will reject it – no matter how pivotal it might be in their lives. This belies the fact "that rational considerations may not, in many cases, be as powerful as other influences in determining the beliefs that human beings hold, reject or revise" (Pekarsky 1994: 128). Religious beliefs can obviously supersede such rationalism.

A secondary assumption of academy is that seeking truth is always desirable. The nuclear bomb, for instance, was the end result of one such inquiry pursued till its practical end (Winchester 1994). It is clear that Abraham Flexner, when he urged the "irresponsible" exploration of ideas, was writing during the pre-nuclear age. A third assumption is that the expression of controversial views is valuable as an end. Exposed to rational debate, an idea may be revealed as valueless. Injury from the expression of controversial ideas is supposed to be ameliorated through a divorce of message and medium. In other words, the "nominally neutral and descriptive 'compare and contrast' mode of presenting basic information ... at least aim[s] to ensure that most partisan expressions of judgement within the classroom are kept in overall balance" (Vine 1992: 173). For the individual actor, liberalism imposes the requirement of "appreciable toleration of judgements and positions that one personally finds misguided or immoral" (Vine 1992: 177). Voltaire incarnate.

In sum, the countervailing principles of neutrality prevent the principle of harm from appearing in the debate. Neutrality allows a liberal to divorce the content of an idea from its source and method of communication, presumably to stand on its own merits in the marketplace of ideas. One might presume, then, that harassment codes are allowable within the liberal vision only if they impose a duty to balance arguments, a position exemplified in the American courts, which have ruled that content-based regulation of speech violates rights guaranteed by the First Amendment.

Liberalism's emphasis on freedom of expression and academic freedom is challenged by religious fundamentalists' contrasting hierarchy of values. Vine makes quite clear at several points (1992: 178, 182, 190) in his examination of religious fundamentalism in British schools that the issues being raised are questions that apply to any group holding its orthodox beliefs against the wider views of the dominant culture. "Like all fundamentalisms ... it takes its body of prescriptive doctrine as revealed truth, and places it beyond dispute and modification" (Vine 1992: 182). Religious fundamentalism is troublesome to liberalism, he would argue, because of the literalist and divine nature of the foundational knowledge structures employed. How, then, can diverse views be reconciled in a socially segmented community such as our universities?

In contrast, arguments for equity are premised on Michel Foucault's demand to account for power. Any examination of how groups, and individuals within groups, are disadvantaged must account for societal hierarchies. For instance, Joanne St.-Lewis (1995) raised the following question around the issue of University of Western Ontario Professor Phillip Rushton: "If we make a PhD a requirement for entry into the debate, at what point do we address economic barriers? If we make a PhD in evolutionary psychology the requirement to debate" asks Professor Rushton authoritatively, "how meaningful is the right to free speech to any one Black person?" In other words, the academy is being asked to recognize that the system under which it operates is not neutral, that when dominant structures are not accounted for, they are re-enforced. The implications of this are many.

For liberals, the paradoxical question is, How can an academy that values tolerance for other cultures accommodate the promotion of cultural values that call for an end to such tolerance? In common parlance, the academy could be forced to put its money where its mouth is and end up losing it all. Harassment policies that purport to promote tolerance do just that and so are bound to this paradox.

Let us turn back to the case at hand to examine possible resolutions. Within the context of liberalism, two possible solutions exist. The dean involved in the case, who must weigh the competing values of free speech and tolerance, could uphold the core value of academic freedom or he could affirm the value of inclusivity on campus, an increasingly responsible act in view of rapidly changing student demographics. Because of the require-ment to either uphold or dismiss the complaint, any other possible deci-sion would simply be a version of one of these alternatives.

To dismiss the complaint, the dean might follow three lines of reasoning. He could decide that no harassment occurred. Presumably the interviews would allow him an insight into the classroom dynamics so as to clarify the reason for this decision. However, the dean has a second option that allows some subtlety. Even if the complaint were to be dismissed, the dean might recognize that the professor had acted in an unprofessional manner but had refrained from actual violation of the policy. The dean might find that some of the comments were discriminatory and had the effect of creating a poisoned environment but that no ill intent was meant. Or, he could dis-miss the complaint by simply accepting the professor's defence of academic freedom. Regardless, the dean must also consider other ramifications of his decisions. For instance, a "clear decision to refuse ... is bound to look like the tyranny of the dominant majority over a relatively powerless minority – something which post-conventional liberals are supposed to recognize as unjust" (Vine 1992: 195). But this is less a consideration because cases of harassment are supposed to be confidential. Only a year-end tally from the harassment office would report the finding of a dismissal. All other details would remain outside the public record of the university.

For the decision to be held in favour of the complainant, the dean would likely have to make some of the following assumptions. He would have to recognize the heterogeneity of students in the class and assume that an instructor's professionalism would not allow the sort of conduct described. That is, the instructor could be compelled to assess the degree of harm any of his comments might have within a diverse classroom. In this circum-stance, the dean would in effect take the position that the collective rights of the class outweighed the individual rights of the professor.

A collectivist concern for minority groups has not been a popular stance in postsecondary institutions. Consider the "Trent University Statement on Free Inquiry and Expression," signed by numerous faculty at that university and endorsed by faculty associations at other institutions. This document affirms the right of members of the university community to "offend one another. It includes the right to express – and the right of access to – intel-lectual materials which express – racially, ethnically, or sexually discrimina-tory ideas, opinions, or feelings, just as it includes the right to expressions that favour inequality of incomes or benefits. It also includes the right to make others uncomfortable, to injure, by expression, anyone's self-esteem, and to create, by expression, atmospheres in which some may not feel wel-come or accepted." So, we are left with the medieval question of whether the one who pays the piper can call the tune (Winchester 1985: 36-7). Within the Trent Statement, both students and taxpayers clearly are being told no. The dominant value of free speech overrules other concerns.

Liberalism tends to deal with clashing rights by creating a hierarchy of such rights, and indeed the policy at this university does so as well. The principle of academic freedom provided a defence for any professor charged with a complaint. In effect, academic freedom trumps equity issues. The dean's final decision mirrored these values and addressed these issues in further detail.

The dean analyzed each of more than one hundred comments and categorized them according to their effect or relevance. The instances of simple swearing were dismissed as outside the jurisdiction of the harassment policy. The references to religion were also dismissed. Criticisms made of Christianity were found to be a legitimate exercise of academic freedom within the classroom. The dean also found this right extended to cover examples in which Christianity was mocked. The dean chose to offer a further warning to the complainant. If the student hoped to function within a secular university, she would have to "get used to it," and should realize that she could not hold others accountable to her moral code.

The dean's decision mimics much of liberal reasoning. Nevertheless, it also raises some difficult questions. Where does a student's freedom to learn enter the debate? What is the role of public education if it cannot accommodate differences? Is religious discrimination different from other kinds of prohibited discrimination because it is more easily changeable than gender or skin colour? At what point are individual rights counterbalanced by individual responsibilities or by collective rights? Stanley Fish raises similar questions (see Chapter 1). He says that religious beliefs are key to understanding academic freedom as an orthodoxy. Religious beliefs are particularly thorny because they are presumably "freely produced." Yet Fish explains that religion and academic freedom vie for the same discursive space. The ground here is particularly thorny because "it is control of education which is the essential basis of any ideology's power" (Vine 1992: 206). Negotiation through each prickly situation is demanded. And yet, the issue of power differentials remains unaddressed in most universities' policies. What we require is a broader vision of regulation.

In any instance, the same action may be understood in different ways: as repressive, as resistant, or as liberating. Therefore policies that focus on acts do not distinguish effects – nor do they account for power. The good intentions of any actor are irrelevant if harm occurs. The harm is real. Therefore, we must develop a new institutional model to address the varying effects of actions or we stand implicated in the same power structures that replicate current inequalities.

I would propose the following to begin the dialogue. If the directly punitive consequences of current policies were to be temporarily sidelined, blame and defensive posturing could cease to act as brakes on dialogue. Discussions of impact might enlighten the debate on rights and turn it towards a discussion of responsibilities. In this way, universities might then move towards becoming learning communities where *all* of us could teach and learn in a broader dialogue.

Fitting final words come from a former president of the University of Winnipeg, who urged us to live with our discomfort: "The difficulty of balancing individual freedom and community only means that there are no full and final answers. Academics, no less than the rest of humanity, find this unsettling; but we should at least be used to it and be able to deal with one another and with cases in a humane and principled way" (Hanen 1992: 22).

**References**

Brubacher, John. 1977. "Academic freedom." In *On the Philosophy of Higher Education*, ed. Brubacher, 39-55. *The Jossey-Bass Series in Higher Education*. San Francisco: Jossey Bass Publishers.

Fish, Stanley. 1997. "Academic freedom and the Inclusive University." *National Conference on Academic freedom and the Inclusive University*. Vancouver: Vancouver Institute Panel and the University of British Columbia. 12 April.

Flexner, Abraham, with a new introduction by Clark Kerr. 1968 [1930]. *Universities: American, English, German*, 3-36. New York: Oxford University Press.

Hanen, Marsha. 1992. "From monologue to dialogue on race and ethnic relations: Creating a climate for institutional change." Keynote panel. *National Symposium for University Presidents on Institutional Strategies for Race & Ethnic Relations at Canadian Universities*. Kingston: Queen's University. 2-4 February.

Newman, John. 1852. *The Idea of the University*. Reprint, Oxford: Claredon Press, 1976.

Pekarsky, Daniel. 1994. "Socratic Teaching: A Critical Assessment." *Journal of Moral Education* 23(2): 119-34.

St.-Lewis, Joanne vs. John Fekete. 1995. A debate on "Academic Freedom and Its Limits." Ryerson Polytechnic University. 16 March.

"Trent University Statement on Free Inquiry and Expression." December 1993-January 1994.

Vine, Ian. 1992. "Moral Diversity or Universal Values? The Problem of Moral Education within Socially Segmented Societies." In *Education for Cultural Diversity*, ed. J. Lynch, C. Modgil, and S. Modgil, 169-209. *Cultural Diversity and the School Series*, vol. 1. London: Falmer Press.

Winchester, Ian. 1994. "Current and Recurring Issues in Post-secondary Education." Class notes. Toronto: Ontario Institute for Studies in Education. June.

–. 1985. "The Concept of University Autonomy: An Anachronism?" *The Professoriate – Occupation in Crisis*, ed. C. Watson, 29-42. Toronto: Higher Education Group.

# 14
# The Inclusive University and the Problem of Knowledge
*Marie Fleming*

My point of departure is that inclusiveness is a good thing. At the same time, I join those who are wary of certain uses of the term "inclusiveness"; for example, when it implies making the university equally accepting of all views, each of which is as good as any other. We cannot allow inclusiveness to degenerate into debilitating relativism, nor let the search for absolute harmony get the upper hand. As a teacher and academic administrator, I have found that too strong an emphasis on harmony and consensus, especially when linked to zealous concerns about subjective feelings, tends to inhibit speech and the healthy spirit of criticism we expect to find at a university. I might not go so far as our Trent University colleagues who claim an academic "right to offend,"[1] but I would say that some "offensive" speech in an academic context is offensive for good reason. The university, as I understand it, should be a somewhat difficult, sometimes exasperating, and always exciting mix of possibilities. It should be agonistic, challenging, and not too comfortable. How can the university be all those things and also be inclusive of the new needs and aspirations that for some years have been making their presence felt on Canadian and other campuses?

I will discuss here why and how we should make the university inclusive. We need to promote a culture of openness, and we need to secure the energetic participation in knowledge of a wide range of social groups. We also have to take the matter of inclusiveness into key areas of epistemological concern. By its nature, the university has to be judged above all by its ability to produce inclusive knowledge; that is, knowledge in the interests of all human beings. Then I will turn to feminist theories of knowledge. These theories successfully challenge the exclusiveness of a male-centred tradition, but they can develop an equally objectionable feminist tradition of exclusiveness.

The tradition of the liberal university obliges us to be open to all sorts of ideas, including those ideas we find unsettling. It also demands that we distinguish between ideas and actions, and that we try not to evaluate ideas in terms of actions associated with them or the persons who put them forth. On the other hand, if we opt too strongly for ideas – valuing them for their own sake and granting them absolute objectivity – then anyone can represent anyone else: it doesn't matter if all the professors are male and white. It's the "objective" value of the idea that counts, and the body of the individual who puts forth the idea – the body, with its desires and needs – is nothing more than a vehicle. This conclusion doesn't fit well with much contemporary research on the relation between ideas and bodies. It is harder and harder to say with any credibility that the body that generated the idea is of no significance. So, it does matter if all the professors are male and white. It does matter if there are no women heading research and teaching. And it matters equally if there are no black professors on campus.

What about the alternative? Should we make sure that the social groups in the university are roughly proportional to those in the general population? We know that the liberal university has historically excluded certain groups from the production of knowledge. For example, women were only indirectly present in knowledge, not present for themselves, not present in their bodies, not agents in the production of knowledge. This situation is one the university should want to avoid. If we work from the presumption of equal participation – if we say that this presumption is essential to liberalism and to the university as a generator of liberal ideas – then the inclusion of previously excluded groups makes the university truly liberal. In other words, the exclusion of identifiable social groups works against the very idea of the university.

There is another reason to strive to achieve inclusion. If the knowledge we produce is related to the producers of knowledge, if the mix of agents changes what is produced, then by shutting out some types of potential producers, we produce less inclusive and therefore worse results from the ones we would have gotten had we been more inclusive. At the very least, we have to assume that the historical absence of certain groups from university life is connected in some significant way to their inadequate theoretical and epistemological treatment. So, even apart from the right to equal participation, we need to promote inclusion to get better knowledge.

However convincing these arguments are, if we go too far in the direction of bodies – if ideas are too closely identified with the persons who put them forward – then ideas are apt to be viewed as congruent with some group's interests. In that event, we stand to lose the core values of the university. At the extreme, we get stuck in group essentialism, where males can only speak for males and women can only speak for women. This conclusion is also false.

What ought we to conclude? Can ideas "transcend" the bodies and experiences of those who have them? Of course. And should we strive for roughly proportional representation of social groups? Of course. Making the university inclusive involves both the effective representation of individuals from a diverse range of social groups and the energetic promotion in the university of openness to ideas associated with ideals of academic freedom.

There are three ways we might work for the establishment of the inclusive university:

1   *Transformation of Institutional Structures.* We should reduce barriers to full participation in university life for individuals from underrepresented social groups. Here, we have to take steps to eliminate personal bias and discrimination. On this matter, I will say only that my own definition of what constitutes personal bias and discrimination is narrow and that affirmative action policies should be adopted and implemented cautiously and with respect for academic freedom.

2   *Promotion of a Culture of Openness.* We should cultivate a university environment in which there is openness to diverse and possibly unfamiliar, even apparently offensive, ideas. If ideas are powerful, we need powerful responses to them, especially if we find them disconcerting. The effective way to deal with powerful ideas is with better and more powerful ideas. We should be reluctant to settle for a weak response (calling in the cops, setting up tribunals, asking for protection, or gagging speakers).

3   *Production of Inclusive Knowledge.* As we develop new and inclusive interpretive frameworks, we need to figure out why and how the university became exclusive in the first place, not only institutionally and historically, but also conceptually. We need to ascertain why what came to be understood as knowledge was exclusive rather than inclusive, as the makers of that knowledge believed it to be. How and why did knowledge that was supposed to be impartial and in the name of all human beings turn out to be partial? We have to deal with the bias that gets scripted into influential theories and thus into what counts as knowledge. That kind of bias, which is not the same as personal bias and discrimination, cannot be easily dealt with.

Anyone taking up the challenge of developing inclusive knowledge will have to start with the ideas of those who have gone before. Even if those ideas are exclusionary, it is not possible to throw them out. We are too embedded in the world, in relationships, in known and unknown needs, desires, and anxieties, to be able to dissociate ourselves from history and the past. New knowledge always transforms what is already there.

We can confront the past in many ways, but in general we can think of ourselves as working from the negative. For example, we can choose some theory that is not inclusive, say how it violates the ideal of inclusion, and explain why the theory or relevant parts of it must be rejected and new directions taken. This strategy is a test for inclusiveness. Inclusiveness is a liberal value.

In many academic disciplines, feminists have applied the test for inclusiveness with much success, as I will discuss below. But can the test be applied to feminist theories of knowledge? That is, is inclusiveness a value in feminist theories as well as in liberal theories? I want to argue that asking these questions of feminist theories brings mixed results. Some feminist theories of knowledge are exclusionary rather than inclusionary.

By now, we have ample documentation of the negative images of women in philosophical, historical, and scientific texts. We also have good reason to suspect that even well-intentioned claims of rationality and impartiality often serve male interests. The question is what to make of such findings. Feminist theorists and philosophers contend that the gender biases and gender-based metaphors in philosophy and science are related to an underlying, masculinist ideal of disembodied subjectivity. The ideal, which generally goes unacknowledged in traditional philosophical and scientific texts, involves a core self, disconnected from human interests and relationships, with nothing to fall back on except its own consciousness. This feminist claim, which I take to be warranted, is significant. It suggests that although philosophers and scientists intentionally strive to understand the world, their ideal of disembodied subjectivity, however obliquely, represents a deep aspiration to escape the dependencies of the world and personal relationships, to become impossibly transparent to oneself, to the point of denying one's own body and emotions. This repudiation of the body, according to feminists, leads to various textual manifestations of the fear of contamination from whatever stands in the way of reaching an impossible ideal. It extends to the repudiation of women, who culturally and historically have been linked with the body and the emotions. If this view is correct, traditional theories of knowledge would appear to reproduce in an abstract form the culturally ingrained gender biases that lead to the gendered divisions of social, cultural, and political life.

The feminist questioning of traditional knowledge extends beyond philosophy and epistemology. Feminists working in social and political theory, literary theory, comparative literature, anthropology, history, political science, visual arts, medicine, and the health sciences and in many of the hard sciences have found patterns of pervasive, deep-seated, gender prejudice. However, the male-centred model that is the target of feminist criticism has not really been left behind, and in the form of an antimodel it continues to drive feminist theories. In rejecting disembodiment and abstraction, feminists thus tend to give value to whatever seems to be undervalued in influential Enlightenment theories: the body, the emotions, relationships, physiological processes.

The limitations of this antimodel of disembodied subjectivity show up in various ways. Insofar as it gives rise to the idea of a "female world" separate from the "male world" and worthy of study in its own right, we find tendencies toward gender separatism rather than progress toward the inclusive university. The problem is also present in feminist analyses of science that identify the objectivity claimed for science with a stereotypically male way of viewing the world and explain the objectivity in terms of male psychosexual development.[2] But the difficulty is particularly conspicuous in relation to the logic of social marginalization that has become a key component in feminist theories of knowledge.

Taken as a group, feminist theories give rise to a basic contradiction: feminists want both to validate women's subjective experiences and to say something "objective" about the world.[3] Given the privileging of women's experiences, the problem is how to justify saying such experiences can be the basis of valid knowledge, which must be inclusive and acceptable to everyone. There are several ways to deal with this problem: deny its importance, assert a need to live with ambiguity and ambivalence, or develop a feminist standpoint theory that gives epistemological and ethical superiority to a group-specific set of experiences and perspectives. Although only a minority of feminists strongly support explicit argumentation in favour of a privileged feminist perspective, almost all feminists promote a concrete "this-worldly" perspective rather than the "other-worldly" perspective of traditional theories. The idea of a "this-worldly" standpoint brings into view the larger questions of validity and privileged perspective taken up explicitly and unsuccessfully in standpoint theory. Thus, to the extent that standpoint theory raises but fails to resolve the issue of privilege in knowledge, that issue represents a fault line in feminist theories generally – even in those that do not explicitly build on standpoint theory.

The core idea of standpoint theory is that privileging women's experiences is analogous to the Marxist privileging of the working class.[4] The basic argument is as follows: the proletariat is socially marginalized, and women are socially marginalized. Therefore, Marxists privilege the experiences of the proletariat in a system of class exploitation, and feminists privilege the experiences of women in a patriarchal sex-gender system.

This argument does not work. In Marxist theory, the proletariat is the agent of history, and as an agent of history the proletariat is inclusive of humanity in that its experiences are the experiences of humanity. For Marx, what matters is not the proletariat's social marginalization but rather the relationship between the proletariat's economic importance and economic exploitation. To be precise, in Marxist theory the proletariat's labour secures the key relationship between surplus value and profit, without which the capitalist system would cease to exist. At the same time, the proletariat as a class has no objectively defined interest in maintaining capitalism, because under capitalist relations of production, the proletariat will never cease to be economically exploited. In Marx's view, the contradictory positioning of the proletariat (that is, its crucial importance and necessary exploitation) suggests an objective basis for capitalism's revolutionary overthrow and points to the possibility of a better future. By contrast, in feminist theory, women's social marginalization is not connected to any centre of economic importance; there is no equivalent to the relation between surplus value and profit. In Marxist and materialist terms, if we cannot show a connection between marginalization and economic importance, we cannot show why women's experiences make women the agent of history, nor why their experiences are interesting or significant beyond their social group, not to mention how we might explain their putative disinterest in the maintenance of the capitalist system.[5]

This situation is not substantially changed by more recent developments in feminist theory. As is well known, there have been numerous charges from black feminists, lesbians, and others that mainstream feminism is grounded in the experiences of middle-class, white, heterosexual women. These charges, which have a valid basis, indicate that feminist theories, like the more traditional theories, have not resolved the problem of privilege in knowledge. However, feminists have been reluctant to address this problem, and in dealing with the issue of white, middle-class, female privilege, have strongly favoured the conservative strategy of making adjustments to existing theoretical frameworks. They have typically tried to expand their theoretical reach, sometimes in concert with the critics within their ranks, by theorizing different types and degrees of marginalization. In general, the argument goes, the more peripheral the group, the more revealing its perspective. For example, claims have been made that lesbians have a vantage point liberated from phallocratic conceptual schemes because they are "outside" the male/female dichotomy.

Feminists have also construed distance from the centre in terms of multiple oppressions. Belonging to more than one socially marginalized group increases the distance from the centre because of the presumably cumulative nature of oppression. The most socially marginalized individuals will be at the farthest point from the centre conceived in terms of intersecting axes of oppression. However, the relation of centre and periphery continues to be a problem.[6] Whereas the socially marginalized proletariat in Marxist theory has a vital connection to the centre of economic and political power, the marginalized group in feminism is always cut off from the centre. The centre of power becomes ever more distant, always somewhere else; there is no hope of capturing it, nor can it be abolished: it is omnipresent and all-powerful, and the marginalized group, however defined, remains forever marginalized.

In the 1980s and 1990s, feminism tended to view class as one further axis of oppression, as an identity that one acquires in addition to other cultural markings such as gender, race, ethnicity, and sexual orientation. Feminism also selects a certain mix of cultural markings – the white, heterosexual, middle-class male – to serve as "oppressor." There can be no solution to the problem of the oppressor,[7] who, as the other of feminism, is an eternal and fixed presence. As the class issue becomes diffused, feminists resort to the generic "men" or "white men" or refer to "dominant groups" or "ruling groups." In the process, the working-class, white, heterosexual male is over-looked. How close is he to the "centre of power"? And is he less socially marginalized than the middle-class, white, heterosexual woman, who by all accounts is the least disadvantaged of the socially marginalized? I don't think so.

Although most feminists might wish to reach out to all the oppressed, it does not seem possible under the social dynamic of groups and the logic of social marginalization to be conceptually inclusive of the economically dis-advantaged. Even affirmative action programs, which are supported by femi-nists, are designed to benefit designated group members who wish to make their way into the middle class.

Feminist theories of knowledge are illuminating and powerful as critiques of a male-centred and exclusive tradition, but those theories are limited as contemporary guides to inclusive knowledge. Despite their rejection of En-lightenment humanism, feminists presuppose that humanity is synonymous with marginalized social groups, and that is why feminists inevitably re-spond with concern to charges by lesbians and gays, Native peoples, visible minorities, and others that mainstream feminist practices exclude them. It is true that feminist theories aim to include marginalized groups and that most feminists actively pursue this aim. Nonetheless, the feminist mode of inclusion runs into difficulty because it is premised on a logic of representa-tion whereby those who are included must identify as victims of male power. But, on the available evidence, feminists in other social groups, for example working-class women and black women, do not experience the feelings of marginalization and powerlessness that are apparently so pervasive among middle-class, white feminists. There is, then, a lack of fit between main-stream feminist theories and the experiences of women who do not share the socially and economically privileged background of the majority of the theorists. As this incommensurability indicates, feminist theories are gener-ally inadequate on questions of class. There is, moreover, a systematic fail-ure to give representation to the interests of white, working-class, heterosexual males. In this case, feminist theories cannot live up to their own ideals of inclusion. As for white, middle-class, heterosexual males, this group is descriptively, normatively, and intentionally excluded from the feminist understanding of humanity. These males are permanently and by definition termed oppressors.

Am I simply pleading for the interests of males? Not at all. I am pleading for my own interests as a feminist. If we want fundamental change, we need a theory that does not get stuck in the margins and does not attribute an otherworldly power to a male establishment. Even as we reject older forms of humanism, we can understand humanity as dynamic and differentiated, not fixed and not reducible. But we must strive to define that humanity as inclusive.

**Notes**

1  The "right to offend" was claimed in the "Trent University Statement on Free Inquiry and Expression," a petition signed by a substantial portion of the faculty and circulated at Trent University in December 1993 and January 1994.

2  Marnia Lazreg, "Women's Experience and Feminist Epistemology: A Critical Neo-Rationalist Approach," in *Knowing the Difference: Feminist Perspectives in Epistemology,* ed. Kathleen Lennon and Margaret Whitford (London: Routledge, 1994), 45-62, suggests that the feminist emphasis on experience and the body locks us into the theoretical dead-end of a subjectivist epistemology.

3  This problem (but not a satisfactory solution) is articulated in Sandra Harding, *Whose Science? Whose Knowledge? Thinking from Women's Lives* (Ithaca, NY: Cornell University Press, 1991).

4  Feminists develop this view by tracing the justification for the Marxist privileging of the working class to Hegel's famous reference to the master/slave relationship. They take Hegel's reference as yielding the insight that more can be learned about society from the life of the slave than the life of the master.

5  I agree with the interpretation of the discrepancies between feminist and Marxist models in Bat-Ami Bar On, "Marginality and Epistemic Privilege," in *Feminist Epistemologies,* ed. Linda Alcoff and Elizabeth Potter (New York: Routledge, 1993), 83-100.

6  For further discussion of the centre/periphery problem, see Bar On, 88ff.

7  I am not convinced by the proposed solution in Harding's *Whose Science?* that men should learn to think and create knowledge "from women's lives."

# 15
## Academic Freedom and Reciprocity: Practising What We Preach
*Jennifer Bankier*

My hope is that we will find ways to work through present conflicts between equity and academic freedom so that groups that have been historically underrepresented in Canadian universities can be fully represented, coexist harmoniously, and achieve their academic potential by exploring diverse interests, philosophies, and goals.

Much discussion has focused on equity conflicts that arise between academics from privileged groups and students from groups that hitherto have been historically underrepresented in our universities (women, Blacks, Aboriginals, Asians, other racial minorities, and people with disabilities) or from groups that historically have been silenced by fear of discrimination (gays, lesbians, bisexuals, and transsexuals). Now, growing numbers of academics[1] from historically excluded groups are present in the academy, and complex disputes over equity and academic freedom can arise among academics from different backgrounds. These may be direct disputes involving academics from equity-seeking groups who allege that they have experienced discrimination from colleagues who are members of historically advantaged groups. Equity conflicts among academics may also arise indirectly as the result of group loyalties that cut across status boundaries within a university. For example, academics who belong to an equity-seeking group may experience retaliation and discrimination if they assist colleagues, students, or support staff from their own group who have raised issues of discrimination with respect to the conduct of academics from advantaged groups.

What I have learned from the discipline and grievance work I have done is that if anything can go wrong in a university, it will, and more lethally than in most other, less politicized environments. Moreover, and unfortunately, many of the resulting conflicts are not simple bilateral disputes involving "virtuous" academics and "evil" administrators, but rather multilateral "member against member" arguments among academics, with administrators joining one side or the other of the dispute. Furthermore, all participants in the argument usually attempt to support their position by making reference to significant academic values (such as equity, academic freedom, procedural or substantive fairness, and academic self-government), with the same values frequently being cited in support of both sides of the dispute.

Despite – or perhaps because of – the growing frequency of these multivalue member-against-member conflicts, I see faculty associations as one of the areas of hope within universities. Faculty associations have strong incentives to encourage reconciliation and to identify strategies that enable their members to live together. The strength of faculty associations lies in the solidarity of their members and their willingness to work together to address matters of common concern through bargaining, lobbying, or other political strategies. Members at war with one another reduce the effectiveness of associations as bargaining units.

To achieve their potential as instruments of reconciliation and resolution, faculty associations must take seriously the concerns of all their members. They must not define political strategy in ways that address only the concerns of historically advantaged groups (for example, senior tenured White men). Such a strategy is politically shortsighted, given the changing demographics of universities in a time of financial cutbacks, an aging professoriate, and early retirement. Faculty associations that today neglect the interests of women, racial minorities, Aboriginals, people with disabilities, and other historically excluded groups because these groups presently constitute a minority of the Canadian academic community may pay a serious price when those groups become a majority of their membership in proportion to their presence in the Canadian population.

These political arguments are reinforced by issues of legality associated with human rights codes and the duty of fair representation that labour law imposes on employee associations with exclusive bargaining rights for their members. Human rights codes bind bargaining agents so that members who belong to groups protected by such codes and who believe that their faculty associations have discriminated against them can file human rights complaints. Labour law's duty of fair representation specifies that faculty associations, like all bargaining agents, must not act in ways that are discriminatory or in bad faith when they represent their members. Legal remedies are available to members whose bargaining agents violate this duty during the grievance or collective bargaining process.

University administrations and faculty associations may tell members of equity-seeking groups to go to a human rights commission or to seek other legal remedies outside the university. In doing so, they attempt to evade their responsibility to create an academic environment that is fair, free, and equitable. This approach is a poor one.

Proceedings in the courts or before administrative tribunals such as human rights commissions or labour relations boards are time consuming and expensive, and the situation is deteriorating as governments reduce funding for courts and administrative agencies. Moreover, external authorities may not understand the complex culture and unique values (such as academic freedom and academic self-governance) of universities. They may therefore arrive at solutions that are not acceptable to any of the academics involved in the dispute. As well, the risk of adverse media publicity increases substantially when those involved in disputes seek solutions outside the university. For all these reasons, we need to develop mechanisms and strategies to effectively resolve equity disputes in the university community.

To identify effective intra-university strategies for reconciliation and dispute resolution, we need to discuss the meaning of our academic values, the relationships, conflicts, and creative interactions among differing values, and the procedures we use to resolve a range of issues within the academy. In conducting this discussion, we must remain aware that although all our values are important, they do not always point in the same direction or suggest a single common outcome in the context of particular disputes. Here, I will develop a broad model for dealing with the creative tensions that exist among academic values inside the university. In undertaking such an analysis, I find it helpful to draw analogies between academic values and certain important social values that play a role in Canadian political life and that appear in the Canadian Charter of Rights and Freedoms – namely, freedom of expression, equity, democracy, and fairness.[2]

To resolve these value conflicts, we could attempt to create one or several primary values to which we would always grant precedence. For example, some individuals would argue that freedom of expression should always win out over competing social values. Others would place equality at the top of the hierarchy. Still others would argue that democracy should always be the dominant value and a Charter of Rights and Freedoms is not a good idea precisely because it constrains the democratic process.[3]

Attempting to ordain a fixed hierarchy of values is a mistake. Rather, it is preferable to recognize that democracy, equality, freedom of expression, and procedural and substantive fairness are all fundamental values both of the larger society and of the academy. The creative tension among them should be resolved not through a permanent declaration of priority that would govern all disputes but rather on a case-by-case basis through decision-making mechanisms that allow the merits and implications of each value to be fully debated in the context of specific disputes involving particular individuals or groups.

In essence, this is the approach that the British and Canadian Parliaments and the Supreme Court of Canada have adopted to deal with disputes among major social values under the Canadian Charter of Rights and Freedoms.[4]

The plaintiff in a Charter case must first establish that rights under one or more sections of the Charter have been violated, after which the defendant (usually a government department) is entitled to argue that under section 1 of the Charter the impugned legislation should survive the challenge because it provides a reasonable limit to the right in question that can be demonstrably justified in a free and democratic society. In arguing that a limit is reasonable in a free and democratic society, defendants can refer to, and the Supreme Court can take account of, important social values such as those that are embodied in other sections of the Charter. By striking a balance between competing social values, the Supreme Court gains the advantage of hearing full and detailed arguments about the significance of these values in the context of specific cases as well as the impact that different decisions could have on both the particular parties and Canada at large.

If the legal system is working properly, the flexibility offered by this case-by-case balancing approach is more likely to produce just outcomes that take into account the diversity of values and needs in Canada than would a system of adjudication that gives priority to only one value. My qualification that the legal system must be working fairly is intended to recognize the reality of power differentials among groups and individuals in Canada. The system will not work properly if one person or group can afford a lawyer to argue its perspective fully before the Supreme Court and those on the other side of the argument cannot do so. Similarly, a fair outcome won't result if those on one side of the debate are so at risk of retaliation from more powerful people on the other side that they fear to take legal or democratic action to assert their needs and perspectives. If we are to have fair, full, and accurate debate about equity and other issues before the Supreme Court, we must take the necessary steps to ensure that all voices that should be heard are present and heard.

The case-by-case balancing approach that the Supreme Court of Canada has applied to Charter cases can be adapted and applied to the resolution of university equity disputes because the four major academic values that may be at issue in such disputes closely parallel the four main social/Charter values. These values are academic self-governance, equality, academic freedom, and procedural and substantive fairness. Although these academic values cannot be enforced using the Charter, they will often be enforceable through other legal mechanisms.

The mechanisms of academic self-governance (senates, faculty and department councils, and appointments, tenure, and promotion committees) are established through a university's governing legislation, internal constitutional documents, and collective or framework agreements.

Academic freedom and equity/nondiscrimination/affirmative action clauses are incorporated in collective or framework agreements and can be enforced through grievance or discipline processes. In some cases, university administrators have put in place employment equity enforcement mechanisms that are separate from collective or framework agreements. Equity claimants also retain the right to seek external relief from human rights commissions.

Fairness rights are often expressly set out in collective or framework agreements. Even in the absence of such explicit protection, administrative law protects the rights of individuals to fairness and natural justice in quasi-judicial proceedings (for example, decisions relating to appointments, tenure and promotion, and discipline).

In universities, as in Canadian society, these academic values exist in a state of creative tension, and conflicts may arise among them. When such conflicts happen, we should look for ways to interpret our governing documents that allow *all* these values to be respected and implemented. In situations where this outcome is not possible, balancing decisions should be made on a case-by-case basis after full arguments by all concerned. To facilitate such discussions, we need to explore more fully the meanings of our fundamental academic values and methods of reconciling them, preferably before we become embroiled in specific, painful disputes where participants lose their sense of perspective and are unwilling to compromise.

In undertaking an analysis of the relationship between academic freedom and equity, it is important to state explicitly our assumptions about the meaning of each of the fundamental academic values.[5] In doing so, there is a better chance that we can identify the roots of our disagreements and thereby move toward shared definitions that will resolve some of our arguments. If not, we at least will understand more clearly why we disagree.

I can illustrate the importance of defining assumptions and concepts through my own analyses of academic freedom and equity. The tensions and conflicts between academic freedom and equity can be reconciled because academic freedom and equity are both designed to address the reality and the legitimacy of differences among individuals and among social groups. For this reason, I can't clearly separate academic freedom from equity and inclusiveness, and you will notice that I interweave them in my analysis.

I will first address the academic freedom issues that arose historically from the lack of inclusiveness in our universities in the purely physical sense; that is, the long-standing absence of representatives of various social groups in Canadian universities. In the past, women, Jews, Blacks, Aboriginals, and other racialized peoples were excluded from Canadian universities. Such exclusion had significant adverse consequences for the members of these groups because universities are gatekeepers: exclusion cut people off from jobs for which education provides an entry.

More importantly, the universities themselves also suffered in terms of their knowledge base. One aspect of academic freedom is the chance to do research, to have time to think and write down thoughts and share them with other people through scholarly writing and teaching. To the extent that Canadian universities excluded Jews, women, Blacks, Aboriginals, other racialized groups, or people with disabilities, Canadian society was denied access to scholarship embodying the expertise, values, and differing perspectives of members of these groups.

Until recently, the professoriate in most academic disciplines was a relatively homogeneous community of White, predominantly European, middle- or upper-class, able-bodied, apparently heterosexual men with shared cultural values. Because these values were universally shared within this limited community, they were assumed to represent universal norms or truths, and they were rarely subjected to serious critical analysis. Under such circumstances, the differences and disagreements most visible in the academic community arose from relatively idiosyncratic, individualized differences in philosophy, values, and personality that were variations on these underlying shared themes. In such an environment, it is not surprising that academic freedom would not surprisingly be perceived as a means of protecting individuals from oppression, and that equality received little attention as an academic value.

Because of its relative homogeneity, the academic community rarely had to pay attention in self-governance or dispute resolution to the more widespread and fundamental differences in values or experiences associated with membership in those social groups or classes that were excluded from or underrepresented in the Canadian academy. As the demographics of Canadian universities change, the academic community must address the reality and the legitimacy of these group differences.

We are starting to make progress in bringing people from historically excluded groups into the universities, where in theory they should have academic freedom and opportunities to share their thoughts, cultures, and values. Yet members of these groups have experienced problems exercising their academic freedom even at the most basic level of the impact of choice of research topic on prospects for tenure and promotion. For example, early female academics were frequently advised to not do feminist research until they got tenure because male colleagues would disapprove and deny them tenure. As the academy continues to diversify through the entry of different equity-seeking groups, Black and Aboriginal Canadians, and other new academics also encounter suggestions that research relevant to the interests and perceptions of their own group isn't "real research" within their academic disciplines.

Constraints on choice of research topics through implicit or explicit threats to job security are the most fundamental kind of violation of academic freedom, yet many academics from historically advantaged groups do not seem to see anything wrong with imposing their own community's research values and priorities on people from communities that do not share them.

Therefore, it is not surprising that members of the historically excluded communities find it necessary to challenge the status quo through grievances or political strategies designed to assert rights to academic freedom and equality.

With the growing presence of colleagues or students with different cultures, experiences, and values, academics from historically advantaged groups have come under pressure as they find that their own values are not universally accepted, their academic analyses and pedagogy are actively challenged by equity-seeking groups, and their power must be shared with people whose perspectives differ significantly from their own. Some historically advantaged academics have risen to these challenges in a constructive manner that respects both the academic freedom and the equity rights of their new colleagues. Others have responded with destructive criticism and defensive attacks on those they see as challenging their authority.

Ideal outcomes for disputes among academics from different groups would recognize that different cultures and values enrich humanity and that universities should therefore welcome the full range of human diversity. In other words, there should be a rebuttable presumption in favour of the legitimacy of difference and of strategies that promote coexistence and mutual respect.

In some situations, it is indeed necessary to resolve differences in favour of a particular approach, either for reasons of convenience (consider the safety benefits of having a law that arbitrarily specifies the side of the road on which all drivers must drive) or because two sets of values cannot coexist side by side (for example, abortion must be either legal or illegal). But before all-or-nothing solutions are adopted, decision makers in Canadian universities should seek solutions that allow people to coexist without violating the integrity of their differing values.

If disputes among equity-seeking peoples and members of historically advantaged groups cannot be resolved through informal intervention such as mediation, and matters proceed to more formal debates through political or legal processes, the arguments will not be restricted to debates over equity principles. In fact, both sides of the debate will often use academic freedom arguments as well. It is therefore appropriate to look more closely at the meaning of academic freedom. One way of looking at academic freedom is as a "reciprocal nonaggression pact" where academics mutually agree that disagreement and personal dislike are not justifications for sabotaging colleagues. I personally subscribe to this definition of academic freedom.

Unfortunately, many academics are not prepared to agree to disagree. Trying to sabotage one's colleagues is a popular academic sport, and it was so long before there were many members of equity-seeking groups in Canadian universities. A large part of a faculty association president's job is to keep the members from attacking each other and destroying one another's careers. I have spent enormous amounts of time pulling the hands of perfectly orthodox traditional White men off the throats of other equally orthodox traditional White men. In the course of an ideological debate or a faculty feud based on personality differences, everyone assumes licence to do in opponents. Criteria for reappointment, tenure, and promotion are so vague that any skilled academic can manipulate them to rationalize getting rid of a colleague for reasons ranging from ideology to personal dislike.

Academics treat each other very badly when it comes to academic freedom. If we are going to make academic freedom a reality in our universities, we have to do better with respect to absolutely everybody, including the members of equity-seeking groups.

If we are ever to have a stable system of academic freedom, we must each take the definition of academic freedom we subscribe to and extend to other people whatever rights of academic freedom we claim for ourselves. I equate this reciprocal extension of the benefits and burdens of our values with principled personal integrity. I respect those who practise integrity with respect to their own definitions of academic freedom – whether or not I agree with the definitions themselves.

Now let us compare the problems that arise from lack of integrity in the application of a couple of models for academic freedom, compared with what these models would require if they are applied with integrity. First, we have the classic liberal model of academic freedom, which states that the cure for speech is more speech. In other words, don't apply regulatory mechanisms to speech, rather have more and more debates. This model is now breaking down because of inequalities of power and a lack of reciprocity in its application. Senior academics who claim that their own critical utterances directed against members of equity-seeking groups are protected by academic freedom use their institutional power to silence members of equity-seeking groups who in turn wish to criticize.

I am talking not only about the problem of the senior scholar who suggests "sympathetically" that research into the concerns of historically excluded groups would not support a successful application for tenure but also about situations where academics and students from equity groups experience vicious personal attacks for speaking out about the harmful consequences that university practices have on their groups.[6]

Think about it. Assume you are leading the way into a new academic unit where no minority members like you have been before. What more important thing would you want to talk about than the need for equity and inclusiveness in the sense of creating an academic environment where you and other members of your group can achieve your full potential as scholars without enduring harmful discrimination? What more important thing could you possibly want to say?

Yet under present conditions, there is a very real risk of retaliation for academics targeted by colleagues who have power over reappointment, tenure, promotion, and research funding. Academics are also remarkably ingenious at making life utter hell on a daily basis for anyone they disapprove of, and this kind of day-to-day hostility saps energy, vitality, and creativity that might otherwise go into academic work. These problems are particularly acute for members of equity-seeking groups who have few allies from their group within their department or university.

The liberal definition of academic freedom, where the cure for speech is more speech, cannot operate properly if "more speech" is silenced or punished through a process of intimidation and retaliation. Either the proponents of this definition should practise what they preach and stand up for the rights of members of equity-speaking groups to criticize and reply to criticism through "more speech," or we need another definition of academic freedom.

What justifications are given for these inconsistencies? Academics from advantaged groups often argue that measures to silence or discredit equity critics are justified because such criticisms are harmful to the careers and reputations of traditional academics. Let us assume, hypothetically, that damage to reputations or careers justifies constraint of academic freedom. Again, this limitation would have to be reciprocal and apply both to members of historically advantaged groups and to members of equity-seeking groups. In return for exemption from criticism that might have an adverse effect on their own reputations or careers, all academics would have to refrain from negative remarks directed against individuals and comments reinforcing discriminatory stereotypes of incompetence aimed at disadvantaged groups in situations where damage to careers or reputations might result.

A reciprocal constraint of this sort would clearly not be acceptable. Academics want to have their cake and eat it too by avoiding any criticism directed at themselves while retaining an unlimited right to criticize others. We will only begin to make progress in our quest for a viable definition of academic freedom when everyone accepts that we must all practise what we preach.

With respect to the definition of equity and the legally enforceable rights associated with it, the Supreme Court of Canada has made it absolutely clear in the context of both human rights codes and the Charter that discrimination is not restricted to situations where there is intent to injure on the basis of group membership. Discrimination can be found in situations where people act on the basis of unconscious stereotypes, and discrimination includes neutral practices that have discriminatory impacts.[7]

"Racism" and "sexism" are simply short names for discrimination on the basis of race or sex, with all the associated legal interpretation and case law.

References to racism and sexism in Canadian universities do not necessarily carry the implication that the person or institution responsible for the behaviour or practice in question is engaging in intentional misconduct. In many contexts, equity complaints are calls for remedial action in the future rather than demands for disciplinary actions directed at particular individuals. This distinction somehow gets lost in debates about equity in Canadian universities.

We all know about "holocaust denial." The academic community is suffering from a bad case of "Supreme Court of Canada denial." What the Supreme Court has said about the requirements of human rights codes and the Charter gets forgotten whenever it is strategically inconvenient for an anti-equity political agenda. It would help enormously if all members of the Canadian academic community could fully comprehend and remember these distinctions between discriminatory intent and discriminatory impact and between prospective and retrospective remedies. If we could achieve this goal, we might avoid many of the major equity controversies of the sort that have arisen in Canadian universities in recent years.

**Notes**

1 "Academics" includes both faculty and librarians.
2 See the Canadian Charter of Rights and Freedoms, Part I of the Constitution Act, being Schedule B of the Canada Act (UK), 1982, c. 11, s. 2(b), s. 3 to s. 5, and s. 7 to s. 15. The Charter does not apply directly to Canadian universities.
3 See, for example, Michael Mandel, *The Charter of Rights and the Legalization of Politics in Canada* (Toronto: Wall and Thompson, 1989).
4 See Peter Hogg, *Constitutional Law of Canada,* 4th ed. (Carswell: Scarborough, 1996), especially 629-30.
5 See also Janice Drakich, Marilyn Taylor, and Jennifer Bankier, "Academic Freedom *Is* the Inclusive University," *Canadian Association of University Teachers Bulletin, Status of Women Committee Supplement* 41 (April 1994): 2-4; republished in *Beyond Political Correctness: Toward the Inclusive University,* ed. S. Richer and L. Weir (Toronto: University of Toronto Press, 1995), 118-35.
6 See Jennifer Bankier, "Vigil Saddens and Reminds Us Inequities Persist," *Canadian Association of University Teachers Bulletin* 42 (November 1995): 7; and Jennifer Bankier, "Trapped Inside the Circle: The Myth of Intent and Resolution of Equity Disputes," *Canadian Association of University Teachers Bulletin, Status of Women Committee Supplement* 43 (April 1996): 4-5, 8.
7 See Maureen Webb, "The Law: What Is Discrimination and How Can It Be Proved?" *Canadian Association of University Teachers Bulletin, Status of Women Committee Supplement* 43 (April 1996): 3, 9.

# 16
# Academic Freedom, Debate, and Bureaucracy

*Lorna Marsden*

Protecting freedom of speech and including people with values and behaviours different from those of the traditional majority are two long-standing struggles in universities. We believe we have a tradition of tolerance, and indeed, we have, but we are apt to jettison that tradition when it impinges on academic privilege. Thus, our strong tradition is also a weakness. Developed in a different age and in a religious tradition where obedience was the norm, Canadian collegiality is often practised as conflict avoidance that reveals itself as a failure to confront the realities of change. Add to this our Canadian penchant for pessimism ("It can't be done") and a perverse sense of inferiority ("It can't be done here"), and we find fragility where, however ambivalently, we long for muscular commitment to change.

University culture is strongly interior: we even build our campuses to confuse with poor signage, inadequate parking, nonsynchronized time schedules, and career lines unlike those in any other industry. Our relations with the world outside the universities are ineffectual: hardly anyone understands that learning, teaching, and research are hard work.

The first duty of a university president is to mobilize the resources that will enable students and faculty to get on with learning, teaching, and research. The second duty is to explain the importance and value of what goes on inside the university to the world outside. If one accepts those duties, one must begin by convincing the university board of governors of them. In the case of freedom of speech, most external individuals and groups accept the importance of the principle and choose on a case-by-case basis to dislike the practice. Thus, the university president must be prepared to defend genuine cases of freedom of speech against the attacks of enraged parents, horrified politicians and business leaders, and titillated journalists.

In the case of inclusiveness, the pressure runs the other way: the enraged groups tend to be the campus status quo, which finds itself challenged and in some cases required to make room for previously excluded groups in residences, classrooms, departments, and common rooms. Even more difficult is the requirement to reorganize the curriculum and course materials to incorporate new literatures, viewpoints, research topics, and types of scholarship. We tend to treat new scholarship as "add-ons" instead of fundamental changes needing to be incorporated in the course material. The victory for feminist scholarship will take place the day it escapes from the confines of women's studies programs and becomes part of the common curriculum.

Outside the universities, the world has resolved the requirements for free speech and inclusiveness largely through bureaucratic means: laws, commissions, tribunals, and administrative practice. In Canada, the outside world now is trying to teach the universities to become inclusive through the same bureaucratic means: employment equity laws, human rights commissions, and other apparatus of the state. All too often, universities are allowing these bureaucratic measures, so inimical to the creative freedoms of scholarship, to supersede legitimate and nonbureaucratic forums such as departmental and senate debates and decision making. Confronted with sexual harassment, many colleagues will try to avoid personal responsibility by saying, "Let the harassment officer take care of it." In other words, these colleagues relinquish to bureaucratic resolution problems intrinsic to the scholarly community. By definition, harassment officers are bureaucrats providing legal solutions often concerned with systemic issues. But not all problems are systemic, and not all suitable remedies are systemic. Individuals can be equally culpable and need to be dealt with as such by their equals. Although systemic inequalities exist and call for rules and special officers, these new institutions should not supplant traditional collegial remedies, such as confronting and resolving a colleague's behaviour. When recourse to harassment officers supplants direct remedies, the larger community loses the authority and creativity of the institution of debate.

Some years ago, Joyce Wieland's "Reason over Passion," a quilt that hung in Canadian prime minister Trudeau's office, became a famous symbol of his style. Reason was the prime minister's passion in his public life. But universities are not "public life." This fact is the strength of universities. We are a powerful mix of the intensely personal ideas and behaviours of scholars and scientists within the context of a public institution. This mix is our strength: we need both reason and passion to succeed. So far, our attempts at inclusiveness have been largely approached by the instruments of reason, such as numerical objectives for the hiring of women and minorities. We have not yet fully accepted these groups on their own terms, which combine all the elements of procedural fairness with a passion for their cause. So, we need to try harder to resolve conflicts and problems of inclusiveness by arguing about ideas, debating and exchanging views face to face, convincing people in debate that we need to change our old ways of dealing with difference.

Debate is a traditional and useful form of authority. To fall back on the old Weberian categories, universities always have lots of charismatic authority at work between faculty and students, but it is their reliance on tradition and on rational-legal forms of authority that needs rebalancing.

A university senate is tradition. Senate is important. It is in the senate that one convinces one's colleagues that changes in curriculum, appointments, and organization are important. Boards of governors, on the other hand, govern more from a legal viewpoint. Accountability is a major issue, audit, performance objectives, and balanced budgets are all the focus of boards. Departments and departmental meetings are equally important. There one can have at one's own colleagues in the language of the discipline, from a deep knowledge of students and of one another, and there, minds can really be changed.

Thus, if freedom of speech means anything, we must have vigorous debates over major issues, and to do that, we must all be able to hear each other. We cannot allow ourselves to be silenced by law and threats of legal action, which brings me to my third and final point. Higher education in Canada is a regulated industry. Like the airlines, the airwaves, or the oil industry, we have regulators who tell us what we will be funded to do. We appear annually in front of the regulatory body – whether it is the ministry or some arm's-length granting council – to beg and explain. Increasingly, those bodies ask for a quid pro quo: Where are our performance measures? Why are so many of our graduates unemployed? Why aren't we responding to industry's demand for more research?

What provincial governments impose is the means of control: in some cases, the number of students the university must admit; in others, the price of tuition. The effect in either case is not only to increase the size of our universities as measured by number of students but also to make a virtue of increasing size. "Bigger is better" is the underlying policy, the assumption being that greater efficiency is achieved by increasing the size of classes, by using technology in teaching, and by giving one university a monopoly over a particular program or discipline. There is no evidence to support this assumption. Indeed, the evidence suggests the opposite.

Given the options, university boards and administrators are caught between the desire to provide a first-rate learning, teaching, and research environment and the need for funding to realize that environment. Thus, instead of offering our students and faculty diversity, we are in danger of offering a series of cookie-cutter universities. This development is not useful to issues of freedom or inclusiveness. To get into university is one thing, but to benefit from it is another. To carry out one's scholarship and teaching takes a different form in small, medium, and large institutions. For most faculty members, whose careers are a "calling" rather than a bureaucratic ladder, these settings and this diversity are important.

With regulations, laws, and budget allocations, government imposes its view of social norms and social order on the university community. The weakness in our universities is that we allow those intrusive measures to replace our traditional institution of debate. We are passive in the face of bureaucracy, and our autonomy crumbles under budget crises and increased enrolments. To survive as inclusive institutions of free debate, we need to restore our departments, senates, and governing bodies: we need to rebalance passion and reason.

# 17
# Regulation or Dialogue
*Dorothy E. Smith*

Recent events at the Universities of Victoria and of British Columbia have involved deep internal conflicts beginning, in both cases, in political science departments and expanding to the universities at large as well as into public discourse. Both have involved critiques of these departments as sexist and, in the case of the University of British Columbia, as racist. Both have brought into play what I am calling "regulatory" discourses: on the one hand, the juridical discourse of accusations, charges, evidence, and due process; on the other, the discourse of academic freedom.

Traditionally, these discourses have been used to defend people's rights against the arbitrary use of state power and the hazard of false accusation, and in a sense more specific to the university, the rights of faculty to teach and write in accordance with their competence and principles, in opposition to the university's central administration and/or board of governors.

Ironically, in the present context these discourses have been deployed to inhibit critical speech, particularly from those in positions of little power (junior faculty and students) when that critique is of racist and sexist practices.[1]

Our universities inherit invisible commitments from a past that excluded women as equals in the creation and transmission of knowledge. Gender organization is in large part historically sedimented and transmitted through local practices passed down over generations. For centuries in Europe, universities were exclusively for men. Knowledge and learning were of men, and men spoke to and wrote for one another. In 1964, Jessie Bernard identified what she called the "stag" effect: when men were asked to name those they held to be significant in their field, they named only men, even when women had done important work. Status within the world of intellectual achievement was male. Men oriented their work to work done by other men, aiming for other men's esteem and recognition. Their everyday working lives were in a world where women were never colleagues. If present at all, women were secretaries, research assistants, sessional instructors, cleaners, food servers, or students. Here was a residue sedimented by an exclusively masculine history.

In the past, men took the maleness of their university and discursive colleagues for granted, and both women and men took for granted the absence of people who could be identified as other based on their skin colour or other physical features. Critiques of racism in the university recover the otherwise shadowy deposits of empire and subjugation in the university's everyday life and the disciplines it reproduces. Universities in Canada were founded in and were integrated with the ruling apparatus of imperial powers that were implicated in the genocidal treatment of the peoples native to the territory we call Canada, institutions of slavery, the subjugation of other civilizations in Africa, India, China, the Americas, and the "Middle East" (the last of these a concept already impregnated with what Edward Said in 1979 called "orientalism"), and the exploitation of the resources of land and people in the subjugated regions. The taken-for-granted white dominance of everyday life is a present deposited by Canada's history of colonialism. Skin colour becomes the present trace of membership in a formerly subjugated people in the context of intellectual and cultural traditions founded in imperialism.

Sociologists (Lee 1996; Sadker and Sadker 1994; Thorne 1994) studying school classrooms give accounts of classrooms where the voices of male students swamp those of girls; boys appropriate the classroom as theirs; girls keep to the periphery and don't initiate speaking with the teacher; the teacher addresses more of his or her remarks to the boys. These aspects of social organization operate at the level of the everyday. And though the everyday social organization of racism is not identical, it also includes exclusionary practices at work in the everyday life of schools and universities. We might imagine an ethnography of a contemporary university department that would display the gender and racialized relations sedimented in the everyday work processes regulated by, but invisible to, the university as a regime. Here is a collection of examples of the kinds of experiences women faculty and students report:

There is a lunch group, all male, all white, at which among other matters, departmental affairs are discussed. Does she get invited? She does not. Does she find herself sometimes in sexually ambiguous situations which institutional differences make hard to handle? She does. An eminent woman professor comes to campus to talk about issues for women in a field that is a major interest in her department. Do the men come to the lecture? No, they do not. Do instructors make comments that draw attention to the colour of her skin rather than responding to what she is saying? Yes, they do. Do instructors sometimes make jokes that single out women as sexual objects in class? Yes. When she speaks up in class or in meetings, do others pay attention? No. Is she called on in class? No. Is she interrupted and displaced when she attempts to introduce topics important to her? Yes.

Once we've been given a language to name them, these experiences are familiar to both white and nonwhite women in universities. For the most part, the experiences do not proceed from deliberate hostility or conscious attempts to exclude. Rather they represent what has come over time to be the everyday texture of working life in universities. Racism isn't found in overtly repugnant behaviours. Nor is racism necessarily intentional. White people are not always conscious of their racism. The language and images (for example, "big bad black bitch," used jokingly to a woman of colour [Marchak 1996: 100]) of Canada's popular culture and intellectual traditions have evolved alongside the expansion and consolidation of European and American imperial projects. Visible distinctions of body type, colour, and eye-shape lock into stereotypes laid down in the cultures and reproduced in media and academic discourse. When a student, a woman of colour, asks a serious question about international relations in the West, and the instructor responds by talking about Africa and Africans, the woman's bodily presence, including the colour of her skin, deflects the instructor's response away from the content of what she said and into interpretive channels determined by the recognition of race. She is dropped from the status of subject in a universalized discourse whose subjects have neither gender nor race. Her voice doesn't count in the same way as the voices of others. In another instance, an instructor approaches a student of African origin (whose family has lived in North America for generations) to say that she wants to be helpful and that she will give the student out-of-class tutoring (Feagin, Vera, and Imani 1996: 95). Given the publication and widespread media discussion of studies purportedly demonstrating the intellectual inferiority of peoples of African origin in North America, the instructor thus unintentionally reminds the student of the attribution of intellectual inferiority and implies that the instructor shares that view.

In the everyday life of universities, the differentiation of race and gender are organized as in-group/out-group relations articulated within the power structure of the university. Of course, there is no longer a perfect coincidence, but the majority of faculty members are still white men, and Jessie Bernard's "stag effect" shows how the in-group/out-group structure excluding women and minorities is also built into the forms of knowledge the structure creates, the discourses in which it participates, and the curriculum it teaches.

In-group/out-group structures may underlie and organize apparently objective representations and accounts. For example, an early twentieth-century map used in surveying the prairies for the purposes of allocating tracts of land to settlers appears objective. It shows roads, railroads, rivers, lakes, towns, and settlements. It does not, however, represent the trails of the First Nations peoples, their settlements, their hunting territories. To take another example from feminist writing: early in the feminist rewriting of Canada's history, an account of women in nineteenth-century Canada used the categories of anglophone, francophone, and Native women. But there is a peculiarity here. Unlike anglophone and francophone, the category of Native women does not designate a linguistically identifiable group. There were different national groups in Canada before the European invasion – peoples of widely varying languages, cultures, economies, and social structures. What the women of these various nations and cultures had in common is that they were *not* the European invaders. The in-group/out-group structure is concealed under an objectifying term that represents the third category as equivalent to the first two. There is an "us" and "them," a subject and an other, buried there.

Characteristically, when people give accounts of experiences they call racist or sexist, they offer a multitude of everyday, apparently minor, incidents. Thus, their critique is of the normal, the everyday, the taken for granted. What history has laid down, we live. "We" do not see the ordinary, everyday forms of oppression, but they do. Feminists use the term "chilly climate" to identify such problems. Each instance may appear trivial, but such instances together articulate distinctive local forms of marginalization. Significantly, those whose everyday and unthinking practices produce these experiences *do not share a consciousness of them*. And generally those who produce for others these exclusionary experiences are in positions of greater power – department chairs, senior faculty, faculty, and so on. Their authority legitimates their version as the institutional reality.

When critiques of racism and sexism are brought forward, they indict the social organization of the everyday working life of a university. The regulatory discourse I have described as "juridical" (Smith 1998) does not capture what is going on at this level. Its language of accusations, charges, and evidence calls for isolating definite, recognizable, and repugnant behaviours – actions that all sides condemn, once they are brought to light. But when each item of the multiple instances that people bring forward as typical of their experience is treated as a discrete incident, an accusation in itself for which evidence must be sought, which must be tested against the recollection of those who performed the act, the character of what has happened disappears: the interwoven character of the "acts" that produce in-group/out-group relations do not resolve into specific local items of behaviour. It is in the nature of such relations that both parties do not experience the incidents in the same way, and the unequal power relations of accuser and accused mean that the "accuser" exposes herself to nonformalized penalties exercised through normal institutional processes.

Neither the chilly climate stories reported by the University of Victoria's political science department's chilly climate committee nor the stories of racism and sexism told by UBC's political science students fit the juridical paradigm. The attempt of the McEwen report (1995) to tell "chilly climate" stories using juridical discourse reveals the fundamental contradiction between the conventions, logic, argumentative procedures, and categorizations of juridical discourse and the essentially interactional dialectic that chilly climate critiques attempt to formulate. At the University of Victoria, senior male faculty insisted that the report of its committee made accusations of sexual harassment against individuals, imposing a regulatory discourse incapable of discovering or expressing the problems and issues that the report attempted to name. Those raising issues were represented as having made accusations of objectionable behaviour against established faculty of good reputation and failing to offer objective evidence for accusations that were for the most part trivial or the result of misunderstanding (for example, Fekete 1994: 294; Marchak 1996: 114; BC Civil Liberties Association as reported by Marchak 1996: 114; Saunders 1995).

By an extraordinary irony, the discourse of academic freedom designed to protect freedom of expression of faculty vis-à-vis the superordinate powers of the university administration has been turned against those in positions of lower power in the university, students and junior faculty who criticize faculty conduct in classes, the content of course materials, and the curriculum in general. The treatment of women and minorities in the classroom, the sometimes savage and irrational treatment of critiques written from antiracist or antisexist standpoints, and the expression of sexist or racist comments in classes have all been linked to general problems of pedagogy in the university. Students have criticized the absence of texts by women or people of non-European origins and of topics recognizing their existence. The discourse of academic freedom is used in a regulatory capacity to fend off such critiques, insisting that they threaten the academic freedom that guarantees professors the right to develop their courses as they see fit.

But in reality, what professors teach is not completely unregulated. Departments do have a say in what courses and topics are taught. From time to time, departments or reviewers from departments elsewhere evaluate programs in terms of current developments in a particular discipline. When such criticisms appear in academic reviews, they are not condemned as infringements of academic freedom. Some department chairs have the right to assign courses and course topics to faculty, and this practice is not viewed as infringing academic freedom. It is certainly not unknown for faculty to criticize the content of another's teaching, and this criticism is not considered as infringing academic freedom. The notion of an essential opposition between academic freedom and the inclusive university suggests that it is not criticism as such that the discourse of academic freedom seeks to inhibit but criticism raising issues of racism and sexism, *particularly issues originating in students' experiences of departmental practices*. The irony lies, of course, in deploying the discourse of academic freedom to repress.

The uses of these regulatory languages conceal and repress dimensions of university life that are consequential to its commitment to rational discourse. The problems experienced cannot be spoken of in the terms and conventions that the regulatory languages impose. Once the categories of regulatory discourses replace the ordinary languages of everyday life that people use to describe experiences of racism and sexism, it is difficult to identify the problem, let alone to discuss remedies.

In general, the institutional processes of universities lack avenues through which problems of everyday sexism and racism can be translated into institutionally recognizable forms for institutional remedy. I suggest that Jürgen Habermas's (1970) formulation of the ideal speech situation as foundational to an ethic of rational discourse offers principles on which such procedures could be built. Habermas holds that rationality, truth, and justice rely on the principles of the ideal speech situation, in which there is symmetry between participants so that each attends to the other, tries to understand and make themselves understood, and tells the truth as they know it. The relationship is reciprocal. Each party is both speaker and hearer, and each recognizes the other as such; there is full mutual recognition of each participant as a subject and a symmetry of the presence of subjects for each other; no single participant is privileged in the performance of dialogic roles. Though one may teach, the other may argue and question.

Derived from the very nature of speech and dialogue, Habermas's ideal speech situation provides a criterion against which the conduct of dialogue can be assessed. In the university, we might want to say, "Yes, this indeed is what academic freedom is about." The concept of the ideal speech situation offers a set of principles to control and subdue our tendencies as academics to believe our own stories and, evading dialogue, impose them on others. As a principle, it imposes a civility that abjures the use of authority to force agreement and insists on reasoning as a method of debate and on the rights of others to question and require evidence.[2]

Theorizing an ideal speech situation as foundational to rational discourse enables identification of conducts that hamper its realization and thus offers principles that take into account what established institutional forms fail to heed. Deformations are imported from "the social structure [external to the speech situation] on the basis of asymmetries in the performance of dialogue roles" (Habermas 1970: 144). For Habermas, rationality is free from the deformations of arbitrary domination, particularly those deformations of which we may not be fully conscious and in respect of which we must rely on others to make us aware. It is clear that the in-group/out-group forms of organizing exclusions based on gender or skin-colour are incompatible with criteria for rational dialogue as specified by the ideal speech situation.

Accounts of experiences of sexism and racism expose deformations of the ideal speech situation that historically have been taken for granted in the everyday working life of the university. To criticize such deformations is not, as Marchak suggests (1996: 16-26; 149), to undermine the very fabric of the university by undermining the claim to objectivity and objective judgment on which the authority of its faculty is based. On the contrary, the role of such criticisms is to discover dimensions of universities that are largely invisible to its established institutional correctives and that injure the university's commitment to rationality, truth, and claims to universality.

Far from threatening the foundations of the university, critiques of racism and sexism are better understood as fully at one with the university's commitment to rational dialogue. They seek to remove deformations in its institutional life that inhibit realization of that dialogue. Historically, these deformations have been sedimented in the working life and intellectual practices of North American universities. Those who make the critique measure the universities' claims to universality and rationality – claims based on an implicit ideal of fully reciprocal and symmetrical dialogue.

The ideal speech situation offers a guide by which we may chart our responses to such critiques. It is part of the nature of the deformations of racism and sexism that we may not be aware how what we take for granted reproduces them. Therefore, we must be open to learning from those who speak from their experience. In entering dialogue governed by the ideal speech situation, both parties must be prepared to risk being changed, to risk being persuaded by the other. One party must not impose on the other interpretations that warp and obscure what he or she is trying to bring into speech. Dialogue implies a serious commitment to listening to the other and to helping the other bring into speech what is sometimes not easily spoken. Rather than responding to initiatives that share our commitment to rational dialogue by imposing regulatory discourses in which they cannot be expressed and that preempt the possibilities of dialogue, we should uphold Habermas's principles of open and rational dialogue. By doing so, we and our critics shall learn and change.

**Notes**

1 The issues addressed in this chapter have been analyzed and discussed at greater length in the context of the events at the University of Victoria in Chapter 10 of my book *Writing the Social: Critique, Theory, and Investigations.*
2 Among other things, the concept of the ideal speech situation puts in question many of the in-practice assumptions of university teaching.

## References

Bernard, Jessie. 1964. *Academic Women*. New York: New American Library.
Bilson, B., and Thomas R. Berger. 1994. "Report of the Review Committee into the Political Science Department." Prepared for the president of the University of Victoria. 21 January.
Feagin, Joe R., Hernan Vera, and Nikitah Imani. 1996. *The Agony of Education: Black Students at White Colleges and Universities*. New York: Routledge.
Fekete, John. 1994. *Moral Panic: Biopolitics Rising*. Montreal and Toronto: Robert Davies.
Habermas, Jürgen. 1970. *Toward a Theory of Communicative Competence*. Inquiry 13: 114-47.
Lee, Alison. 1996. *Gender, Literacy, Curriculum: Rewriting School Geography*. London: Taylor and Francis.
Marchak, Patricia M. 1996. *Racism, Sexism, and the University: The Political Science Affair at the University of British Columbia*. Montreal and Kingston: McGill-Queen's University Press.
McEwen, Joan I. 1995. "Report in Respect of the Political Science Department of the University of British Columbia." Vancouver: University of British Columbia.
Sadker, Myra and David Sadker. 1994. *Failing at Fairness: How America's Schools Cheat Girls*. Don Mills: Maxwell Macmillan.
Said, Edward W. 1979. *Orientalism*. New York: Vintage Books.
Saunders, Doug. 1995. "Ruffled Feathers on Campus." *Globe and Mail* 1 July: A1, A3.
Smith, Dorothy E. 1998. *Writing the Social: Critique, Theory, and Investigations*. Toronto: University of Toronto Press.
Thorne, Barry. 1994. *Gender Play: Girls and Boys in School*. New Brunswick, NJ: Rutgers University Press.

# Contributors

**Jennifer Kate Bankier** was born and raised in Hamilton, Ontario, and holds a BA from the University of Toronto (1970) and an LLB from Osgoode Hall Law School of York University (1974). After teaching for three years at Wayne State University Law School, Detroit, she went to Dalhousie Law School in Halifax, Nova Scotia, where she is currently an associate professor. She teaches in the areas of torts, women and law, trusts and estates, law and technology, intellectual property, and American constitutional law and has done research on equity and academic freedom issues in universities, law and computers, and class actions.

A current member of the executive of the Canadian Association of University Teachers, Bankier chaired the CAUT Status of Women Committee, and she has also been president of the Dalhousie Faculty Association and chair of the DFA Grievance Committee.

Jennifer Bankier is coauthor (with J. Drakich and M. Taylor) of "Academic Freedom *Is* the Inclusive University," published in *Beyond Political Correctness: The Canadian University in the 21st Century,* eds. S. Richer and L. Weir. Her numerous publications include articles on equity themes in the *CAUT Bulletin,* such as "Debating Academic Freedom and the Inclusive University," "Trapped Inside the Circle: The Myth of Intent and Resolution of Equity Disputes," and "The Subtleties of Silence Can Be Deafening: Social Justice Debates Should Not Be Derailed by Inappropriate Use of Silencing Rhetoric."

**Stanley Coren** is currently a professor of psychology at the University of British Columbia with degrees from the University of Pennsylvania and Stanford University. Coren's research has covered many areas of psychology, including human vision and hearing, neuropsychology, brain laterality, birth stress, sleep, and cognitive processing. His research has resulted in the publication of well over 300 articles in scientific journals such as *Science, Nature, The New England Journal of Medicine, American Journal of Public Health, British Journal of Medicine,* and *Psychological Review.* He has also published twenty-two books, monographs for professionals, and textbooks for students. One of these is the textbook *Sensation and Perception,* which has now gone into its fifth edition and has consistently been the most used college text in North American courses on sensory and perceptual processes.

Coren's research has earned him election as a Fellow of the Royal Society of Canada. Much of his research has caught the attention of the popular press and the electronic media. His findings on lifespan and handedness, sleep deficits in contemporary society, and dog intelligence has resulted in several best-selling books. For instance, *The Intelligence of Dogs* has been translated into twenty languages. He has appeared in many national TV and radio programs, both in the United States and in Canada.

**Diane Dyson** is a doctoral student in the higher education group, Department of Theory and Policy Studies, at the Ontario Institute for Studies in Education. Her research centres on the negotiation of difference within the university.

Dyson completed her undergraduate work in political science at Concordia University. Her institutional incarnations have included student advocate, student activist, and student journalist. These experiences have inspired her academic quests. She is also a single mother of two children, Kay Elizabeth and David Jupe.

**John Fekete** is Distinguished Research Professor of Cultural Studies and English Literature at Trent University in Ontario. His work is in Anglo-American and European literary and cultural theory, including problems in modernism and postmodernism; Hungarian and North American science fiction, including Utopian narratives and the horizons of the technological imagination; and, finally, social psychopathology in popular culture, including moral panic and censorship.

Fekete has published four books: *The Critical Twilight* (1978), *The Structural Allegory* (1984), *Life after Postmodernism* (1987), and *Moral Panic: Biopolitics Rising* (1994). He has also published numerous scholarly articles.

**Stanley Fish**, dean of the College of Liberal Arts and Sciences at the University of Illinois at Chicago, holds a BA from the University of Pennsylvania (1959) and an MA (1960) and PhD (1962) from Yale. He has taught at the University of California at Berkeley (1962-74), at Johns Hopkins University (1974-85), where he was the Kenan Professor of English and Humanities, and at Duke University as a professor of English and of law.

His earliest work centred on late medieval literature (1400-1536) and was especially concerned with the relationship between rhetorical manuals and various generic forms. In 1964, he began publishing in the area of sixteenth- and seventeenth-century nondramatic literature (prose and poetry), with special attention to the writings of John Milton and George Herbert and to the relationship between aesthetics and theology. In 1969, he became attracted to new developments in linguistics and literary theory and produced several studies keyed to the notion of the structure of "reader response." This research led, in the 1970s, to an interest in the institutional processes by which readers are constituted as well as to the formulation of a new account of development and change under the rubric of "interpretive communities."

In 1980, his attention was called to parallel developments in legal theory, and he has now extended his researches into that line of inquiry. He continues to write on and lecture in all of the fields noted above. From 1994 through 1998, Dr. Fish assumed duties as executive director of the Duke University Press.

**Marie Fleming** teaches political philosophy at the University of Western Ontario and from 1992 to 1997 served as director of Western's Centre for Women's Studies and Feminist Research. Her interest in research and teaching began in St. John's, Newfoundland, where in 1965 and 1969, she earned undergraduate degrees in education and classical studies from Memorial University. Her postgraduate education was completed at the London School of Economics and Political Science, where she graduated with an MSc (Econ) (1972) and a PhD (1976).

Fleming has published extensively on nineteenth-century French anarchism, contemporary German philosophy, and feminist theory. She is the author of *The Anarchist Way to Socialism* (1979), which appeared in a revised edition titled *The Geography of Freedom* (1988), and *Emancipation and Illusion: Rationality and Gender in Habermas's Theory of Modernity* (Penn State University Press, 1997). Her current research includes two projects: one dealing with critical theory, modernity, and art; the other with feminism, reason, and the academy.

**Graham Good** has taught in the UBC English department since 1971 and specializes in critical theory, nonfictional prose, European literature, and modern British fiction. *The Observing Self,* his study of the essay from Montaigne to Orwell, was published by Routledge in 1988. A concern with the erosion of liberal and humanistic values in the university is reflected in his essays "Northrop Frye and Liberal Humanism" (*Canadian Literature* 148, Spring 1996), "The Hegemony of Theory" (*University of Toronto Quarterly* 65.3, Summer 1996), and "Facecrimes," a review of the McEwen report on the political science department at UBC (*Literary Review of Canada,* October 1995). His book *The Betrayal of Humanism: Theory, Ideology and Culture in the Contemporary University* is forthcoming from McGill-Queen's University Press.

**Michiel Horn** was born in the Netherlands and in 1952 came to Victoria, BC. After working for the Bank of Montreal, he entered Victoria College, the University of British Columbia (BA history and English 1963), attended university in Freiburg in Breisgau, Germany, and did graduate work at the University of Toronto (PhD 1969). He has taught history at Glendon College of York University since 1968, has chaired the Glendon College history department, and has also been associate principal (finance) of Glendon College, as well as chair of the York University Faculty Association.

His services outside York University include member, Canadian Association of University Teachers Executive Committee; member, CAUT Academic Freedom and Tenure Committee; treasurer, Ontario Confederation of University Faculty Associations; and chair, OCUFA. Since 1976, Horn has been academic coordinator, Living and Learning in Retirement, Toronto.

His publications include *The Dirty Thirties* (1972), *The League for Social Reconstruction* (1980), *A New Endeavour* (with Frank Scott, 1986), *Academic Freedom* (1987), *Becoming Canadian* (1997), and *Academic Freedom in Canada: A History* (1999). His current project is *A History of Ontario* with Roger Hall of the University of Western Ontario.

**Jennie Hornosty** is professor of sociology at the University of New Brunswick. She holds a BA from the University of California, Berkeley, an MA in sociology from Dalhousie University, and a PhD in social and political thought from York. She is currently a member of the President's Task Force on Creating a Positive Learning and Working Environment. Recently, she completed a two-year, part-time secondment as employment equity educator for faculty. Her teaching areas include the sociology of women, feminist theory, sociological theory, and contemporary debates in sociology, while her major research interests are violence against women in farm and rural communities, the impact of violence in the home on the workplace, and the different assumptions underlying principles of equity and equality.

Actively involved in the Association of the University of New Brunswick Teachers (AUNBT), Hornosty was president from 1989 to 1991 and served on the CAUT national executive as member-at-large from 1991 to 1994. She was a member of the Joint UNB-AUNBT Employment Equity Committee for six years.

Her publications include "Balancing Principles of Equality, Equity and Diversity with Academic Freedom," in conference proceedings from *National Conference on Women, Culture and Universities: A Chilly Climate?* (Sydney, Australia, 1995), and "A Look at Faculty Fears and Needed University Policies against Violence and Harassment," in *Violence: A Collective Responsibility*, 1994 SSFC Symposium on Violence.

**Sharon E. Kahn** has been a professor of Counselling Psychology since 1975 and has concentrated her research on counselling theory, gender-fair practices, and women's career issues. In 1989, she became the University of British Columbia's first Director of Employment Equity. Under her guidance, the equity program she inaugurated has received two Certificates of Merit from the federal government. In 1997, UBC also received a Vision Award from the federal government in recognition of the quality of the University's employment equity program.

In 1994, Kahn was appointed UBC's first Associate Vice President, Equity. In this new position, she became responsible for administering the university's employment equity and educational equity programs and for its handling complaints of discrimination and harassment.

Her publications, which appear in Canadian, US, and international books and journals, address the interests of both scholars and practitioners. In 1993, she co-edited (with Bonita C. Long) *Women, Work, and Coping: A Multidisciplinary Approach to Workplace Stress.*

**Lorna Marsden** was born and raised in Sidney, BC. She holds a BA from the University of Toronto (1968) and a PhD in sociology from Princeton University (1972). From 1982 to 1992, she was a senior fellow at Massey College, University of Toronto, where she remains as a continuing fellow.

Now president of York University, she was president and vice chancellor of Wilfrid Laurier University from August 1992 to 1997. Previously, she served for twenty years at the University of Toronto as professor in the department of sociology and in several administrative positions. From 1984 to 1992, she also served as senator in the Parliament of Canada, representing Ontario. In the Senate, she chaired the Standing Committee on Social Affairs, Science and Technology, and served on the National Finance Committee and on the Banking, Trade, and Commerce Committee.

Her research has been in the area of social change in Canada, encompassing the areas of labour force and labour market analysis and population issues. She has a particular interest in the circumstances of women in economic life and in social movements. Her books include *The Fragile Federation: Social Change in Canada* (with E.B. Harvey), *Lives of Their Own: The Individualization of Women's Lives* (with Charles Jones and Lorne Tepperman), and eighty other articles on the labour force, gender issues, and work and occupations.

Marsden has received honorary degrees from the University of New Brunswick (1990), the University of Winnipeg (1994), the University of Toronto (1995), and Queen's University at Kingston (1995).

**Dennis Pavlich** is the University Counsel at the University of British Columbia and in that capacity is a member of the President's Executive Team. He is a professor of law with special interest in the areas of real property law, the law of trusts, education law, and condominium law, the subject of two books he has authored. He also has publications in a number of academic journals.

A graduate of Witwatersrand University and Yale Law School, Pavlich has taught law for over twenty years. He has also lectured extensively to groups concerned with higher education law. On two occasions he was awarded the Faculty of Law's annual prize for teaching excellence, including the Killam Prize. He has served on the Senate of the University of British Columbia, its Board of Governors, and is a former president of the UBC Faculty Association. He sits on the boards of several university-related organizations.

**Stan Persky** teaches philosophy at Capilano College in North Vancouver, BC, and is a book columnist for the *Vancouver Sun*. He is the author of several books, including *Buddy's: Meditations on Desire* (1989), *Then We Take Berlin* (1995), and *Autobiography of a Tattoo* (1997). He is also the co-editor of *The Supreme Court of Canada Decision on Abortion* (1988), author of the introduction to the edition of the Supreme Court of Canada decision on Aboriginal land claims, *Delgamuukw* (1999), and is the coauthor of *On Kiddie Porn: Sexual Representation, Free Speech and the Robin Sharpe Case* (forthcoming).

**Judy Rebick** is one of Canada's best-known feminists and political commentators, and is the host of *Straight from the Hip,* a CBC Newsworld talk show. She was also cohost of *Face Off,* a nightly TV debate show. She is author of *Imagine Democracy* (Stoddart, 2000).

Rebick teaches a women's studies course at the University of Toronto and writes a column for *Elm Street,* a national women's magazine. The author of numerous articles on women's issues and a lecturer on a variety of issues across the country, she has also coauthored (with Kiké Roach, a young black feminist) the book *Politically Speaking* (1996).

From 1990 to 1993, Rebick was president of the National Action Committee on the Status of Women, Canada's largest women's group with more than five hundred member groups. In 1993, she led a grassroots opposition to the Charlottetown Accord. When she was president, NAC helped to win a stronger rape law and refugee status based on gender persecution as well as to defeat a new abortion law. In 1994, Rebick was a visiting professor in political science at the University of Regina. She was then a regular political commentator on national radio and television. Until September 1996, she was also a lay member of the Ontario Judicial Council, the body responsible for adjudicating complaints against provincial court judges in Ontario.

Over the past twenty years, Judy Rebick has also been an active supporter of people with disabilities. She worked as director of special projects for the Canadian Hearing Society from 1980 to 1991 and was co-chair of Disabled People for Employment Equity.

**Frederick Schauer** is Frank Stanton Professor of the First Amendment and Academic Dean, John F. Kennedy School of Government, Harvard University. The holder of AB and MBA degrees from Dartmouth College and a JD from Harvard University, he was a trial lawyer for two years before embarking on an academic career in 1974. After teaching at West Virginia University from 1974 to 1978, he became Cutler Professor of Constitutional Law at the College of William and Mary, and he was professor of law at the University of Michigan from 1983 until 1990, when he assumed his current position. He has also served as visiting professor of law at the University of Chicago (1990) and at the Harvard Law School (1996, 1997, 2000), and as Ewald Distinguished Visiting Professor of Law at the University of Virginia (1996).

Teaching and writing in the areas of constitutional law, freedom of speech and the press, the philosophy of law, and legal constraints on policy making, Schauer is the author of *The Law of Obscenity* (1976), *Free Speech: A Philosophical*

*Enquiry* (1982, awarded a certificate of merit by the American Bar Association), and *Playing By the Rules: A Philosophical Examination of Rule-Based Decision-Making in Law and in Life* (1991). He is a founding co-editor of the journal *Legal Theory* and is coauthor of *The Philosophy of Law: Classic and Contemporary Readings* (1995) and *The First Amendment: A Reader* (1991, 1996). His writings include many articles in legal and philosophical journals. He served as chair of the Section on Constitutional Law of the Association of American Law Schools, was vice president of the American Society for Political and Legal Philosophy, and was elected a fellow of the American Academy of Arts and Sciences in 1993.

In recent years, he has held distinguished lecturer positions at Dartmouth College, Macalester College, Georgetown Law School, University of Connecticut School of Law, University of Wyoming College of Law, Australian National University, and University of the North in South Africa. He has also been involved in projects on constitutional and legal development in Estonia, Mongolia, South Africa, Australia, Taiwan, and Belarus and has lectured on legal and constitutional transformation in Chile, Spain, New Zealand, Hungary, Israel, Finland, and Canada.

**Bernard Shapiro** became the principal and vice chancellor of McGill University in 1994. Born and raised in Montreal, where he earned his undergraduate degree from McGill, he received his doctorate in education from Harvard University in 1967 and joined the faculty of Boston University, where he later became associate dean of the university's School of Education. He returned to Canada in 1967 to become dean of the Faculty of Education at the University of Western Ontario, and two years later he was appointed vice president (academic) and provost of that university.

In 1980, Shapiro moved to Toronto to assume the position of director of the Ontario Institute for Studies in Education, a post he held until 1986, when he was appointed deputy minister of education for Ontario. Since then, he has also served as deputy minister of skills development, deputy secretary of cabinet, deputy minister and secretary of management board, and deputy minister of colleges and universities. In 1992, following his retirement from the Ontario public service, Shapiro joined the University of Toronto as a professor of education and public policy.

He is past president of both the Canadian Society for the Study of Education and the Social Science Federation of Canada. He has also served on the executive committee of the International Association for the Evaluation of Educational Achievement and, in Paris, as chair of the governing board of the Centre for Educational Research and Innovation.

Shapiro is the author of numerous articles on curriculum, public policy in education, the development of logical thinking in young people, and educational research and methodology. He has addressed provincial, national, and international educational organizations in Canada and abroad, and has received honorary degrees from McGill University, University of Toronto, University of Ottawa, McMaster University, Yeshiva University, Université de Montréal, and University of Edinburgh.

**Harvey Shulman** is professor of political science, and principal, Liberal Arts College, Concordia University, where he teaches political theory and Western civilization. His publications have been primarily in politics and the Bible, and the intersections of Jewish and Western political thought. He has a growing research interest in academic freedom and the university curriculum.

In 1978, he participated in the founding of a great book program at the Liberal Arts College and became vice principal and principal for twelve years. Shulman is vice president of the Concordia University Faculty Association and serves on its negotiation team.

His publications include "Bible and Pedagogy in the Teaching of Western Civilization" (*Jewish Political Studies Review*), "Israeli Democracy: Some Thoughts" (*Middle East Focus*), "The Political and the Sacred: Political Obligation and the Book of Deuteronomy" (*Jewish Political Studies Review*), and "The Bible and Political Thought: Daniel J. Elazar's Contribution to the Jewish Political Tradition" (*Judaism*).

**Dorothy E. Smith**, after working as a secretary for a number of years, did a degree in sociology, specializing in social anthropology at the London School of Economics. Graduating in 1956, she and her husband (William R. Smith) entered the doctoral program at the University of California, Berkeley. She completed her doctoral degree in 1963. Divorced in 1965, she moved in 1968, with two small sons, to teach in the department of anthropology and sociology at the University of British Columbia. In 1977, she left UBC to join the department of sociology of the Ontario Institute for Studies in Education.

She records three major shifts in her thinking: first, attending the London School of Economics at the age of twenty-six and becoming fascinated with sociology; the second, at Berkeley, where she was deeply influenced by Tamotsu Shibutani's interpretation of George Herbert Mead, by reading the phenomenology of Maurice Merleau-Ponty, by the anti-Vietnam War student movement, which was very active on campus at the time and, perhaps most important, by the Canadian women's movement, which became a site of personal transformation, political activism, and a profound rethinking of established sociology.

Since she became active in the women's movement, her work as a sociologist has been preoccupied with finding out how to research and write the social from women's standpoint. Her thinking and research are worked out in a series of books, papers, and reports, including an edited volume with Sara David, *Women Look at Psychiatry* (1975), *The Everyday World as Problematic: A Feminist Sociology* (1987), *The Conceptual Practices of Power: A Feminist Sociology of Knowledge* (1990), *Texts, Facts and Femininity: Exploring the Relations of Ruling*, and *Writing the Social: Critique, Theory, and Investigations* (1998). Her current research and theoretical work in the field of institutional ethnography aims to explicate the role played by texts in institutional forms of action.

**Lynn Smith, QC**, was formerly a professor of law and dean of the Faculty of Law at the University of British Columbia. She holds an Honours BA in philosophy from the University of Calgary and an LLB from the University of British Columbia. Her academic writing is in the areas of the Canadian Constitution, human rights, evidence and civil procedure, and health policy and law. She was editor in chief of *Righting the Balance: Canada's New Equality Rights* in 1985 and was coauthor with Professor William Black of the chapter on equality rights in the last two editions of *Canadian Charter of Rights and Freedoms* (Beaudoin and Ratushny, and Beaudoin and Mendes, eds.). She is coauthor of *Civil Jury Instructions* with the Honourable Mr. Justice John Bouck.

Smith has been involved over a number of years in university and professional committees that attempt to address issues of discrimination and noninclusion. She participated in various governmental policy formation exercises such as the National Forum on Health and the Korbin Commission on the Public Service and the Public Sector. Smith was active in continuing judicial education programs, including the Western Judicial Education Centre's program on gender and Aboriginal equality issues. She was a member of the board of the Law Foundation of British Columbia for seven years and its chair from 1996 to 1998. She served on the board, and as chair, of the BC Women's Hospital and Health Centre from 1994 to 1998.

Smith left the University of British Columbia on her appointment to the Supreme Court of British Columbia on 23 June 1998. The Honourable Madam Justice Smith continues to be a member of the board of the National Judicial Institute, which provides continuing education programs for the Canadian judiciary.

# Index

Set in Stone by Artegraphica Design Co.

Printed and bound in Canada by Friesens

Copy editor: Maureen Nicholson

Proofreader: Terry J. Vieth

Indexer: Patricia Buchanan